Stay Smart!

Smart things to know about... is a complete library of the world's smartest business ideas. **Smart** books put you on the inside track to the knowledge and skills that make the most successful people tick.

Each book brings you right up to speed on a crucial business issue. The subjects that business people tell us they most want to master are:

Smart Things to Know about **Brands & Branding**, JOHN MARIOTTI
Smart Things to Know about **Business Finance**, KEN LANGDON
Smart Things to Know about **Change**, DAVID FIRTH
Smart Things to Know about **CRM**, DAVID HARVEY
Smart Things to Know about **Customers**, ROS JAY
Smart Things to Know about **Decision Making**, KEN LANGDON
Smart Things to Know about **E-Business**, MICHAEL J. CUNNINGHAM
Smart Things to Know about **E-Commerce**, MICHAEL J. CUNNINGHAM
Smart Things to Know about **Growth**, TONY GRUNDY
Smart Things to Know about **Innovation & Creativity**, DENNIS SHERWOOD
Smart Things to Know about **Knowledge Management**,
    TOM M. KOULOPOULOS & CARL FRAPPAOLO

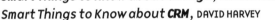
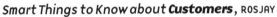

Smart Things to Know about **Leadership**,
    JONATHAN YUDELOWITZ, RICHARD KOCH & ROBIN FIELD
Smart Things to Know about **Managing Projects**, DONNA DEEPROSE
Smart Things to Know about **Marketing**, JOHN MARIOTTI
Smart Things to Know about **Partnerships**, JOHN MARIOTTI
Smart Things to Know about **People Management**, DAVID FIRTH
Smart Things to Know about **Scenario Planning**, TONY KIPPENBERGER
Smart Things to Know about **Strategy**, RICHARD KOCH
Smart Things to Know about **Teams**, ANNEMARIE CARACCIOLO
Smart Things to Know about **Your Career**, JOHN MIDDLETON

You can stay **Smart** by e-mailing us at **info@wiley-capstone.co.uk**
Let us keep you up to date with new Smart books, Smart updates, a Smart newsletter and Smart seminars and conferences. Get in touch to discuss your needs.

CAPSTONE

INSTANT · KNOWLEDGE

Smart
THINGS TO KNOW ABOUT

Leadership

JONATHAN YUDELOWITZ

RICHARD KOCH

ROBIN FIELD

The rights of Jonathan Yudelowitz, Richard Koch and Robin Field to be identified as the authors of this work has been asserted in accordance with the Copyright, Designs and Patents Act 1988

First published 2002 by
Capstone Publishing Limited (a Wiley company)
8 Newtec Place
Magdalen Road
Oxford OX4 1RE
United Kingdom
http://www.capstoneideas.com

CIP catalogue records for this book are available from the British Library and the US Library of Congress

ISBN 1-84112-113-4

Typeset in 11/15pt Sabon by
Sparks Computer Solutions Ltd, Oxford, UK
http://www.sparks.co.uk
Printed and bound by
T.J. International Ltd, Padstow, Cornwall

This book is printed on acid-free paper

Substantial discounts on bulk quantities of Capstone books are available to corporations, professional associations and other organizations. Please contact John Wiley & Sons for more details on 212 850 6000 or (fax) 212 850 6088 or (e-mail) info@wiley-capstone.co.uk

For Archbishop Desmond Tutu
whose leadership has turned hatred into forbearance and love
and shown South Africa and the world
that everyone has a story
and the chance to exercise personal leadership and responsibility
in their own unique and individual way.

Contents

What is Smart?

The *Smart* series is a new way of learning. *Smart* books will improve your understanding and performance in some of the critical areas you face today like *customers, strategy, change, e-commerce, brands, influencing skills, knowledge management, finance, teamworking, and partnerships.*

Smart books summarize accumulated wisdom as well as providing original cutting-edge ideas and tools that will take you out of theory and into action.

The widely respected business guru Chris Argyris points out that even the most intelligent individuals can become ineffective in organizations. Why? Because we are so busy working that we fail to learn about ourselves. We stop reflecting on the changes around us. We get sucked into the patterns of behavior that have produced success for us in the past, not realizing that it may no longer be appropriate for us in the fast-approaching future.

There are three ways the *Smart* series helps prevent this happening to you:

- by increasing your self-awareness;

- by developing your understanding, attitude and behavior; and

- by giving you the tools to challenge the status quo that exists in your organization.

Smart people need smart organizations. You could spend a third of your career hopping around in search of the Holy Grail, or you could begin to create your own smart organization around you today.

Finally a reminder that books don't change the world, people do. And although the *Smart* series offers you the brightest wisdom from the best practitioners and thinkers, these books throw the responsibility on you to *apply* what you're learning in your work.

Because the truly smart person knows that reading a book is the start of the process and not the end ...

As Eric Hoffer says, "In times of change, learners inherit the world, while the learned remain beautifully equipped to deal with a world that no longer exists."

David Firth
Smartmaster

Acknowledgments

We enjoyed writing this book, and finished up even better friends than we started. So we would like to thank each other.

We may not have seen further than earlier writers, but we have been able to put together the first broadly based view of business leadership.

Our main influences fall into three distinct categories:

- psychologists and other professional writers on leadership;

- writers with unusual insight into how business success is created, and who have written about leadership because they realize it is crucial to making money; and

- writers who are neither experts in emotional intelligence, nor in business, but who have pondered the human condition and provided terrific clues about the meaning of life and how we can influence ourselves and other people to create **progress** and how we can each reach our **individual and unique destiny**.

In the first category fall Dr I. Adizes, Eric Berne, Warren Bennis, Robert Eccles, Richard Erskine, Mary Parker Follett, Dr Peter Hawkins, Elisabeth Henderson, Robert Kramer, Marion Milner, Dr Arnold Mindell, Nitin Nohria, Jeffrey Pfeffer, Carl Rogers, Myrna Wajsman-Lewis, and Margaret J. Wheatley.

Our greatest business influences here are Edward de Bono, Andrew Carnegie, Charles Handy, Bruce Henderson, Bob Noyce, and Jack Welch.

In the third category of wise writers, we'd like to specially mention Hans Christian Andersen, Lyman Frank Baum, Martin Buber, Winston Churchill, Viktor E. Frankl, Benjamin Franklin, F. Scott Fitzgerald, James Gleik, Jacob and Wilhelm Grimm, George Orwell, Ayn Rand, William Shakespeare, George Bernard Shaw, Oscar Wilde, and Virginia Woolf.

You'll meet all these people in the book – we hope with as much pleasure as we experienced.

Finally, great thanks to Mark Allin and Richard Burton, our publishers, and to our families, colleagues, and close friends.

Ultimately, this is a book about **business** leadership and how to **make money** through exerting leadership. But along the way, a necessary first step is to consider **who we are** and how we can make the **most difference to the world**. Only if we crack these difficult but rewarding issues can we be **successful**, and, more importantly, **happy**.

So **enjoy**. There is much to savor and chew over here. It is our pleasure to bring you concentrated wisdom and knowledge about leadership – and some real emotional challenges too.

1
Leadership Demystified

"I'm all for progress; it's change I don't like"

Mark Twain

Why leadership?

The point of leadership is to initiate change and make it feel like progress.

It's not just Mark Twain who was against change. We all are. But where there is life, there is change. Change is inevitable. The issue is whether we are going to be hapless victims of change, or initiators and exploiters of change, for the benefit of ourselves and of other people. Are we going to suffer change, or drive progress?

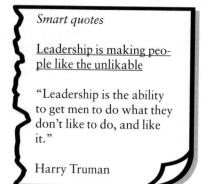

Smart quotes

Leadership is making people like the unlikable

"Leadership is the ability to get men to do what they don't like to do, and like it."

Harry Truman

Leadership is what takes us and other people into a better world. Leadership insists that things must be done differently. Leadership rides the forces that are pulling individuals, groups, organizations, markets, economies, and societies in different directions, and lends a coherence that will enable us to benefit from the change around us. Leadership says, "We cannot just carry on doing what we have done before. See all these forces of change around us; they are not just threats, they are also opportunities. But we must do this rather than that."

If it is effective, leadership persuades people who would otherwise carry on doing what they are doing, to do something different, in accordance with a shared view of what that "something different" comprises. Leadership uses change to make progress.

Smart answers to tough questions

> Q: Isn't the idea of progress dead?
> A: Yes and no. Philosophers and historians no longer believe that life is an ever-upward path – there is plenty of evidence to the contrary. Yet business and science have combined to create a near-utopia that would have been inconceivable three centuries ago. Economic growth at 3% a year means that wealth doubles within 23 years. Over a century there is an increase of 20 times. Business leadership drives this growth – which makes poor people rich.

Leadership is a quality, a culture, a role, a mind-set, and a set of actions. Leadership encompasses everything that is necessary to induce constructive change.

What is a leader?

The real definition of a leader is someone who provides such leadership. This person, these people, who are true leaders may or may not be the formal leaders. There may be no formal leaders. The group itself, which is experiencing and benefiting from leadership, may not even be defined to start with.

What this book can do for you – leadership to create wealth

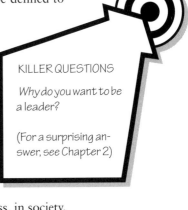

KILLER QUESTIONS

Why do you want to be a leader?

(For a surprising answer, see Chapter 2)

This is a book for both formal leaders – those whose job it is to lead – and for informal leaders – those who lead regardless. For both current and aspiring leaders.

Yet our focus is on *business leaders* and *business leadership*. There are many common factors to leadership in business, in society, in politics, and in other theaters. But one of the requirements of leadership is a good instinct about what to do. It is no use persuading people to change if you get them to do the wrong thing. Change would then not be progress; it would be "anti-progress." The instincts about what to do require specialization.

Q: If business leadership is different from leadership in general, why do nearly all leadership books and courses draw on examples of political and military leadership?

A: Examples are always useful and business examples are always tricky. The business leader may go through a bad patch after the book has gone to press. Another reason is that most of the people writing about leadership are psychologists and organization development specialists whose understanding of "leadership" is greater than their understanding of business and how to make money. This book will draw on general insights about leadership and what drives individuals to self-knowledge, but also on how this can be used specifically to create wealth.

Smart answers to tough questions

In business, leadership is not just about making things different and better. It is about making money in the process: lots of it. This is the only objective test as to whether resources are being used sensibly, whether change really is economic progress. We want to tell you how to use leadership to make lots more money.

KILLER QUESTIONS

Do you want to be a leader or a business leader? Why?

Moving from the present to the desired future

This entails understanding the environment, and one's own and others' motivations, (in all their complexity), deciding on future direction, and mobilizing people in that direction.

Smart quotes

Leadership is proving the unprovable

"Most leaders in some deep sense are striving to prove something which is unprovable."

Gerry Robinson

Business leadership is about effective and profitable adaptation to the conditions around the organization: it's about choices and actions that are mindful, sensible, and yet courageous too. Taking and executing decisions in a way that is responsive and flexible, as well as deliberate and influential, that makes sense to colleagues, and gains commitment from them.

Business leadership must distinguish hype from healthy optimism; denial and over-skepticism from prudence. The leader must be able to judge when it is time to act; how to frame strategies in order to appeal to others and get things going.

In so doing the leader manages the boundary between what *is* happening – the present – and what *needs to* happen – the desired future – taking into account the group's legacy and position: its potential, dreams, obstacles and prejudices.

Leading is living and influencing

We all take such leadership decisions throughout our adult lives – in our choices of career or life-partner, whether or not to have children, to move home, start a business, or change jobs. In none of these situations can a management system or glossily packaged pop-psychology provide a definitive, sustainable answer. Instead, we have to face reality, choose and act, in time, with no guarantee that we have done the right thing.

Leadership in business is like that, with the additional complication that deliberate change has to result from the impact that people have on each other.

Think about the person who has influenced you most in your life, who despite your anxiety and regardless of receiving no reward and risking punishment for non-compliance, got you to risk and act on an idea, in a way that you would never otherwise have done.

> *Smart quotes*
>
> <u>Leadership is moving people to the unknown</u>
>
> "The task of the leader is to get his people from where they are to where they have not been."
>
> Henry Kissinger

Think of another case where, because of someone else's influence, you decided to move beyond your usual range of behavior, so that you were able to achieve something you would never have dreamed possible without their encouragement. The effect these people had, what they represented for you, the things they said, and how they conducted themselves – sharing your triumphs and joy, supporting you through uncertainty and failure – are what leadership is all about.

Leadership is about <u>you</u>

Very few of these leadership qualities can be developed through accessing others' writings or courses. Erudite authors have published thousands of books, and the holy texts of most world religions deal extensively with the topic of leadership. Yet intellectuals, theoreticians and religious people don't necessarily make the best leaders.

Why? Because competence in leadership is fundamentally rooted in *who one is*, rather than in *what one knows*.

Think of leadership as having two components: a general component; and a specific component, which is dependent on the context in which you happen to be operating at any particular time. The general component relates to *who you are*; the specific component to *what you know* about business and the specific opportunities and threats facing any enterprise. Many people can know a great deal about the latter without being effective leaders. If you doubt this, just go to any strategy consulting firm and talk to its 20-something consultants.

Although knowledge and skill are vital, it's one's integrity, self-esteem, resilience and other personal qualities that count for most when it comes to leadership.

Chains of command and management systems may create compliance and conformity – but lasting purposeful change, which feels like progress, is a function of leadership; based on the fundamental, age-old principles of judicious wisdom, strong relationships, integrity, mutual trust and respect, and an ability to manage oneself in the moment.

Smart answers to tough questions

The paradox of corporate uncertainty

Almost by definition, organizations can only join people together through concerted, focused effort by all their people. This requires the alignment of decisions and the mobilization of common actions amidst a diversity of human interests, uncertainty, and ever-changing environments. The larger the organization and the more varied the markets, the more this complexity, diversity and uncertainty are compounded – and the more difficult it is to join people together in the first place.

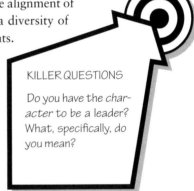

KILLER QUESTIONS

Do you have the *character* to be a leader? What, specifically, do you mean?

The laws of physics tell us that every action has its reaction, each having equal significance and value. For instance, ask any leader or group of leaders in a big company to list their strategic imperatives and one will notice that before one page is filled, the items begin to contradict one another.

What complicates things further, is that often one imperative makes equal sense to its opposite, and seems just as beneficial to the organization. Take *customer service*. Several books in the "management fad" section of a typical airport bookstore will argue that customer loyalty is paramount, and one's sales force will chant that the "customer is king," and go on to insist

Smart quotes

Leaders embrace uncer-
tainty

"Leaders must place them-
selves squarely in the zone
of discomfort and learn to
tolerate ambiguity."

Richard Pascale

that his demands should be sacrosanct because "he pays one's salary."

That seems simple enough; yet as Oscar Wilde said, "the truth is rarely pure and never simple." If we ask the opinion of a manager concerned with organizational efficiency, he will tell you that giving in to customer demands costs money, and can therefore negatively affect the bottom line, compromising both shareholder interests and well thought-out policies and procedures which have been designed to eliminate favoritism and to ensure efficiency and fairness through uniform treatment for all.

Should such a tension lead to a quarrel between customers and staff, and for argument's sake, one takes the customer's side over an employee's – particularly when that employee was applying a policy or procedure in what he understood to be the company's best interests – one is risking being seen as inconsistent and damaging staff morale and of violating the principle that "our people are our greatest asset," which is, according to umpteen other books, absolutely true.

Every senior executive has faced dilemmas such as this, where he has had to mediate a dispute between various competing interests, all of whom have had "a piece of the puzzle," but are each presenting information and arguing credibly to outmaneuver one another and "win the day." How do we resolve such an issue?

Kaplan and Norton introduced the notion of *"The Balanced Scorecard"* – an organizational management system that aims to give equal weight to human/social imperatives (which promote growth and learning), organizational efficiencies (business processes), customer needs, and financial requirements (or those of shareholders who are looking for financial returns).

They propose that one can engineer *logical systems* to manage organizational dilemmas, and that with appropriate management rigor and discipline, one would achieve a *balanced*, effective, and efficient organization.

KILLER
QUESTIONS

- If you want to be a leader, are you sure you can cope with the inherent uncertainty and ambiguity?
- Can you cope with the conflict that leaders always experience?

But Kaplan and Norton brushed over the fact that trading-off between opposing points of view and imperatives is always challenging and requires presence of mind, level-headedness, a strategic view, and integrity. This is especially the case when one cannot calculate the right answer – both because each side seems believable and the future is uncertain, and when one suspects but cannot prove that the rational arguments are presented merely to further personal interests.

Furthermore, it's not just a matter of making a decision; leaders must also ensure it makes sense to everyone. Process Oriented Psychology teaches that an interest group or person who feels discounted or under-acknowledged by a decision will resist it, either passively (working-to-rule and passing on information only when asked), or actively (overt sabotage). Leaders need to know how to provide intelligent, integrated solutions to company dilemmas, in which everyone will at least acquiesce.

Smart quotes

A full life means a life full of contradictions

"Everything comes alive when contradictions accumulate."

C. Bacheland

We may be told that all imperatives – short-, medium- and long-term, staff-, customer-, public- or shareholder-related – are equally important. In specific situations, however, leaders must favor one over another. The specific trade-off will depend on the information available, the risks and benefits of each action, what will make the most money, the ethics of treating people fairly, and on the particular message the leader chooses to send to the organization.

Of course it is beneficial to have a comprehensive management system that tracks and measures achievement of conflicting financial and non-financial business objectives and aligns initiatives accordingly. Yet, human beings still need to make sense of the conflicts, agree on their implications, and trade off and take decisions to ensure progress. Effective leaders work *with* the paradox of uncertainty, and so embrace fundamental tensions, supporting and listening, challenging, and directing in a holistic and integrated way.

The yin and yang of leadership

Such conflicts are linked, at a deeper level, to the fundamental universal tensions that Jung called *anima* and *animus* (female and male archetypes), and that Taoists refer to as *yin* and *yang*.

Smart quotes

Creation requires androgyny

"A mind that is purely masculine cannot create any more than a mind that is purely feminine … the androgynous mind is resonant and porous; it transmits emotion without impediment; it is naturally creative, incandescent and undivided."

Virginia Woolf

Working with *yin* and *yang* requires a certain type of thinking. An androgynous mind can strategize and inspire, energize and arouse the lethargic, and defuse the panicked and hostile. An effective leader knows when to apply the maxim "don't just stand there, do something" (be action oriented) and when to use its opposite, "don't just do something, stand there" (be patient, contemplate, and be reflective).

Being smart is being schizo

"The test of a first rate intelligence is the ability to hold two opposed ideas in the mind at once and still retain the ability to function."

F. Scott Fitzgerald

Leaders must be mindful, able to see all sides, and be decisive, flexible and mature in deciding who is right in each a situation; what will create the most wealth. To create clout, leaders must also, sometimes, use drama and surprise.

Be mild and thump the table

"Leaders often combine consensus building with another somewhat contradictory technique – occasional public and drastic displays of their strong support for new ways of doing business."

Charles Farkes and Suzy Welaufer

Management versus leadership

Managing means planning, organizing, directing, controlling, and monitoring in order to get things done and to attain a clear, defined set of objectives.

Smart quotes

The trap of management rationale

"A man has his beliefs: his arguments [management rationale] are only excuses for them. Granted that we both wanted to get to Waterloo Station: the question whether we shall drive across Westminster Bridge or Waterloo, or whether we shall walk across Hungerford foot bridge, is a matter for logic; but the destination is dogmatic. The province of reason is the discovery of the means to fulfil our wills; but our wills are beyond our reason ... our temperamental convictions produces oversight as to all the facts that tell against us."

George Bernard Shaw

It is largely about marshalling resources towards achieving a desired out-come: achieving or winning according to a particular paradigm or set of rules. An unfortunate and unintended consequence of this is that management systems themselves tend to reflect the assumptions held by the managers who designed them. Furthermore, people management (performance management, reward and recognition etc.) systems encourage people to place a "spin" on facts in order to make things look good; to enhance their own or their manager's ego and reputation so as to reinforce the notion that everything is under control and going according to plan, even though this may be far from the case.

Smart quotes

Managing the past

"Most management practices are designed to monitor the past rather than create the future."

Tony Manning

Many well-managed organizations have gone out of business because they failed to see beyond their assumptions.

Management is inherently conservative. Psychological theory and in particular the transactional analysis theories of Berne and Erskine explain how people will naturally protect their assumptions about the world in order to feel in control when faced with stress or challenge.

Leadership, in contrast, faces up to things as they really are rather than as we want them to be, regardless of how it makes us, our boss, or our organization look. It involves being aware of our assumptions, questioning them, and *working out the right things to do and doing them.*

Managers achieve objectives; leaders work to a purpose

Leaders can discern patterns amidst the apparent chaos of the business environment and envision a desired future state and possibilities, often with little or no supporting data. To see the real picture, leaders must be able to screen out their own bias.

Real progress requires an ability to let go of one's own comfort zones and assumptions, which may mean hearing or seeing what one does not want to

Leadership is a calling

"Change is almost always accompanied by controversy, discomfort and resistance ... which forces leaders to rise above their natural inclinations ... requiring people to lead in ways inconsistent with their personalities... Leadership is therefore much more of a calling than a management style."

Charles Farkes and Suzy Welaufer

Choice is uncertainty

"If choice is real, the future cannot be certain. If the future is certain, there can be no choice."

Brian Loasby

hear or see, to take courageous decisions, and engender the necessary trust amongst others to do the same.

Even worse, we cannot hope to consistently make the right decision first time. If the waters are uncharted, we're bound, sooner or later, to get lost.

The leader must therefore change or abandon a strategy if it's not working, regardless of how this may affect the organization or her own image or ego. Whereas the manager sets out to achieve objectives, the leader aims to fulfill a purpose – *a specific and unique way* to create long-term wealth *that fits one organization perfectly.*

The idea of the cause

In 1907, Henry Ford announced that his company's mission was "to democratize the automobile" – to make something that was the preserve of the rich affordable to ordinary working men. That was a cause. In the nineteenth century, the unification of Italy, and of Germany, were causes. The elimination of starvation and of smallpox are causes. To grow into the leading supplier of a particular product or service is a cause. Becoming larger than a much bigger competitor is a cause. Providing the world's best ideas for business is a cause.

To excite people, and to create a sense of future momentum and direction, good leaders use *causes*. A cause is something that needs doing to create progress. It is the purpose that will mobilize a group of people – an organization or a tribe within it – to do great things.

A cause is something that needs doing. If nothing needs doing, and if nothing new is done, there can be no progress.

In selecting a cause for your group, follow these guidelines:

- Adopt a *unique* cause. If someone else already has the cause, why should this excite people or cause them to follow you?

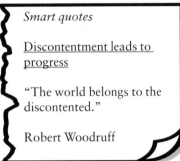

- Ensure it's an *exciting and worthwhile* cause.

- But also that it's *attainable* within a reasonable time period – usually between one and five years.

- The cause must *fit your people, your firm or unit's history and its capabilities*. The cause should fit your unit better than it would fit any other unit. Otherwise, other firms or groups will be better placed to carry out the cause. Another reason to ensure this close fit is that you will not excite people unless they can see why *they* are uniquely qualified to execute the cause – if they don't believe this, they will be turned off.

- The cause must *fit you*. Otherwise, it would better suit another leader. The cause must be something that you are personally passionate about. You can't manufacture this – synthetic excitement is soon seen through. The cause must be totally congruent with your personality, skills, and motivation.

Developing the right cause is often a difficult and non-linear process. Do not rush it. Evolve it. Use trial and error to see whether an incipient cause really does suit you and your people. Don't proclaim the cause very emphatically until you are sure it is right – and it has a good chance of being realized.

Smart quotes

Purpose gives joy

"This is the true joy in life, being used for a purpose recognized by yourself as a mighty one; being a force of nature instead of a feverish, selfish little clod of ailments … complaining that the world will not devote itself to making you happy."

George Bernard Shaw

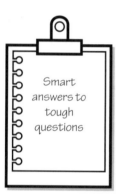

Smart answers to tough questions

Q: Is a "cause" the same as a "mission" or a "vision?"

A: A cause is essentially the same as a mission but different from a vision. We prefer the word "cause" to "mission" because the latter sounds too "religious" and is very difficult to translate from English to other languages.

A "vision" is different from a "cause." A cause is what the organization (or part of it) is going to do. A vision is what the organization could become.

A cause is always very specific and usually has a fairly short time fuse. You will always know whether your cause has been attained or not. Once your cause is fulfilled, you'll invent another cause.

A vision is fuzzier, longer term, and longer lasting. You cannot really "reach" a vision. It is qualitative and not quantitative. It is an aspiration, an emotion, a dream.

Visions are extremely useful to leaders. We'll discuss visions later in this chapter. When we do, remember that the cause and the vision, though different, must be congruent and complement each other.

Ultimately, though, you must have a cause. If you are trying to make change feel like progress, you need to know what "progress" really means.

Don't plan the future

A leader has to make sense of how the future is unfolding, in order to decide how to act now and communicate a vision of the future that will carry the group there.

But in thinking of the future, beware. Many nasty traps await you.

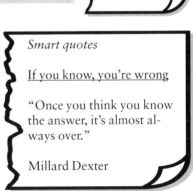

Markets cannot be predicted

"The complex phenomena of the market will hardly ever be fully known or measurable, unlike most of the factors that determine events observed in the physical sciences."

Friedrich von Hayek

Smart quotes

Organizations, and societies run by organizations, tend to be blind to the future, because they have such a strong vested interest in keeping the present running. The collapse of Nazism, communism, and apartheid are extreme but instructive examples. Talent, energy and money were channeled in to prop up these systems – maintaining the present in respect of past assumptions – rather than towards change and progress – confronting the boundary between the present and the future.

Smart quotes

If you know, you're wrong

"Once you think you know the answer, it's almost always over."

Millard Dexter

Leaders must stand aloof from their organizations' tendency to deny that the future will be different. An opposite trap lies in a subculture within organizations, happily not so prevalent as fifteen or thirty years ago, but still present or lurking below the surface – the idea, much beloved of marketers, finance people, MBAs, and unreconstructed strategists, that the future can

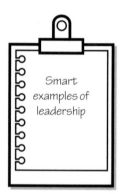

Smart
examples of
leadership

HOW LEADERS CAN GET LOST IN SPACE

James Gleik, in his recent book, *Faster*,[1] watches the first episode of the 1965 American television series *Lost in Space*, which was an inter-galactic adventure set in the far future – 1997.

"So there on the screen, photographers are milling around in Alpha Control to capture this historic 1997 moment, and flash bulbs pop. Yes flash bulbs. Remember them? Actual bulbs that fired once, smelled of burnt metal and had to be replaced for the next shot? Now the view pans back from an image of the galaxy distantly displayed on a giant mock-up of a giant 1965 television set – the round corners are a dead giveaway. The control-room walls are lined with vintage 1965 computers: refrigerator-sized cabinets with flashing lights and large reels of tape. In fact everything looks absurd and bulky and somehow slow – the big old-fashioned television cameras rolling about with their cables trailing behind; even the lights (no miniature LED's). The mission engineers work at desks that seem to be equipped with big switches and bulky knobs and flashing lights of their own – but, you can't help but notice, no keyboards, no mice, no display screens. And what are those shiny round disks resting on the desks of this advanced, high-tech, space-mission control room? Ashtrays … Who can guess what new materials, what new fashions, and what new devices will betray this year's science fiction when another generation has passed; or what new social behaviour: no one guessed, a generation ago, that a 1997 control room would be a no smoking zone."

The program predicted convenient moon travel and machines that washed, dried and ironed clothes in 16 seconds, breakthroughs that seem as fantastic now as in 1965.

be planned or predicted with tolerable accuracy. You can tell these people by their dynamic energy, their sheaves of printouts, their luminous presentations, their enthusiasm, and their utter sense of conviction. They are dressed for success, yet their siren songs will surely lure you to perdition. Fire them all immediately.

Vision

Though the future abounds with paradox, it is so uncertain and complexly determined that enterprises that fail to take responsibility for their future are unlikely to endure. The key tool is some *vision* of the firm and its future.

Vision provides a sense of meaning and aspiration that can never be fully described. Nevertheless, all effective visions have a *fundamental* resonance and clarity that will make sense, encourage, and also provide discipline.

Vision is usually described as a destination – a picture of where the organization should be going, and of how you define success in the future. True, but not the whole truth. As befits a holistic and invisible force, vision simultaneously describes the present, the past, and the future; what the organization is as well as what it should become; what drives the enterprise as well as where it will drive; what gives it power; why it deserves a place in the economy; what it has done and will do for the world.

Smart quotes

Take the future in small doses

"It's a mistake to look too far ahead. Only one link in the chain of destiny can be managed at a time."

Sir Winston Churchill

Smart quotes

Expect the opposite

"Expect what you do not expect."

J M Coetzee

Smart quotes

Vision is invisible

"Vision is the art of seeing things invisible."

Jonathan Swift

We have to describe a vision in words, but they need not be – generally, should not be – too precise. A dream must be fuzzy. If we enjoy the dream, awake and try to make sense it, to tie it down to terms we can fully understand, then we drive it away. The dream is not something we fully understand, yet it is a force we can feel, and it can drive us forward in a way that a plan tightly based on words and numbers never could.

Smart quotes

Vision is a holistic dream

"To carry on a successful business a man must have imagination. He must see things in a vision, a dream of the whole thing."

Charles M. Schwab

If vision is about behavior and ideals, then it matters hugely whether the "chief visionary" – the leader – embodies these ideals and behaviors. Vision is visceral, not rational; emotional, not intellectual; personal and personalized, not dispassionate. The vision must be *congruent* with the leader, and the leader must be congruent with the vision.

We come back to the indissoluble link between the leader's effectiveness and the leader's integrity. Who the leader is, what she feels, what she thinks, what she says and what she does, need to be congruent. The vision, validated by the leader and what she stands for, needs to "hold together," give hope and meaning – feel true to individuals, teams and organizations over long periods of time, and in various different situations.

Smart quotes

Ideas control

"It's the ideas of business that are controlling, not some manager with authority."

Robert Haas

Successful leaders use language artfully to describe their vision; people feel that despite not always being able to see the possibilities it suggests, they are still able to suspend their anxiety and disbelief. They follow their leader into uncharted territory because they trust him or her, and therefore the vision itself.

In describing a vision, leaders face a challenge similar to that of the great artist. The leader has to describe some-

Vision is power

"Vision is a field [as in scientific field theory] … in creating a vision, we are creating a power, not a place, an influence, not a destination … we need congruency in the air, visionary messages matched by visionary behaviours … vision must permeate throughout the whole organization as a vital influence on the behaviour of all employees."

Margaret J. Wheatley

thing coherent, realistic and unifying, but sufficiently complex to provide hope and meaning to a diversity of people, interest groups and professions in a way that stands the test of time.

The vision is not necessarily a new idea; instead the leader is able to sense what needs to happen next, to synthesize and explain with credibility.

Vision is effective fantasy

"Many great strategies are simply great visions. And great visions can be a lot more inspirational and effective than the most carefully constructed plan. Only when we recognize our fantasies can we begin to appreciate the wonder of reality."

Henry Mintzberg

Virginia Woolf described how Tolstoy and Shakespeare had affected her world-view: "One holds every phrase, every scene to the light as one reads – for nature seems, very oddly, to have provided us with an inner light by which to judge of the novelist's [leader's] integrity or disintegrity."[2]

Following this analogy, the thing about leaders is how they sense the not-always-obvious connections between things. In the words of the great existentialist philosopher and author, Arthur Koestler, "the leader uncovers, selects, reshuffles, combines and synthesizes." The leader responds creatively to his or her environment, "sorting the signals from the noise ... seeing the picture emerging from the mist" and describes a dream for the future in a way that inspires commitment, restraint and action and which bounds anxiety and uncertainty. Good leaders use their sense of future together with expert intuition and interaction with people to keep things on track – giving meaning to setbacks and triumphs alike.

KILLER QUESTIONS

Leaders have a *cause* and a *vision*. What are yours? Are they different yet congruent and complementary?

Conclusion

To recapitulate our key points:

- Leaders translate change into progress. Progress implies a clear idea about what is to be improved – the leader's *cause*. The cause must be specific, verifiable, unique, and fit the organization and the leader uniquely well.

- Leadership has a generic component. Leadership competence is fundamentally about who you are; your character. "Strong" character is not enough. To be a leader, you must have an unusual and paradoxical combination of self-worth and self-doubt, awareness of self and of others, and the simultaneous ability to belong and to be detached.

- Leaders must be able to deal with uncertainty, ambiguity, trade-offs, and conflict. Leaders have androgynous minds, combining and alternating between female and male archetypes.

- Leadership is fundamentally different from management. Management means running things as efficiently as possible under existing policies and objectives. Leadership means changing direction as conditions evolve, working out the right things to do and persuading other people, usually against their inclinations, to change course. Management is the "government" or executive; leadership is the "opposition" or campaign agitator. Yet leaders have to get results too – through the power of persuasion rather than through the power of hierarchy.

- Although leaders have to take us into the future, they should eschew trying to plan or predict it. Leaders evolve their ideas as conditions change. Leaders are infinitely flexible and often inconsistent. Yet leaders still manage to convey a sense of where we are going, even though they have little more idea than the rest of us of how the future will unfold. How do they manage this? Through vision – a view of things that are invisible but visceral, imaginary yet real, influential though intangible.

- Leadership depends on the particular situation. Leaders need to belong and be accepted, as well as having the skills to work out where to take a group. This means that an excellent leader in one situation or time may be hopeless in another. "Fit" is everything.

- Business leadership is different from other forms of leadership, because an enterprise has a different character and role in life than, for example, an army or a government or a voluntary organization. Creating wealth is a different vocation from creating other forms of well-being. A business leader must be a specialist in money-making as well as having good general "leadership" skills – otherwise he or she will not be an effective leader.

In other words, business leadership is tricky! It's marvelous, but it's not what people think it is. It's no wonder that great business leadership is so rare. It's not so much that it is any more difficult than anything else worthwhile, but that conventional views of leadership are so far from the truth.

In the next chapter, we review the controversies about leadership, before describing in the rest of the book the "anatomy of leaders" – a detailed review of the psychological make-up, qualities, and behavior of business leaders.

Notes

1   James Gleik (1999) *Faster*, Random House, New York.

2   Virginia Woolf (1929) *A Room of One's Own*, Hogarth Press, London.

2
Leadership Wars

Before plunging into our account of how effective leaders behave – which will come from Chapter 3 onwards – we want to clear up some popular misconceptions about leadership. We also want you to know where we stand on key debates about leadership – and what the other views are.

Is leadership all hype and no substance?

"Now that I'm CEO, what am I supposed to do?"

"You're supposed to make superficial statements about how good the company is, then hope something lucky happens and profits go up. It's called leadership, sir."

So says Dilbert, the Scott Adams creation. One of the evident problems with leadership is that anyone can have an opinion about it. What makes one person's opinion better than another person's? And if it's all a matter of opinion, is there any real substance behind leadership?

Is leading an army the same as leading a corporation or a group of scouts? And if not, then is "leadership" as a generic description an illusion?

Our view is that if you divorce leadership from real life issues, then it is hype. We shouldn't try to think about leadership out of context. Leadership is *not* a great human quality. It is *not* a generic and wonderful attribute. Leadership is a *skill*, different from other skills, which is more necessary in some situations than in others. Leadership is a *function*, an activity that is useful, but only if we define the objectives.

If we want to conquer the whole of Europe and impose the will of what we believe is the master race on all other human beings, we need a different kind of leader, and a different type of leadership behavior, than we do if we want to make a small firm into a large and successful corporation.

Leadership is only good if you share the leader's objectives, or if they share yours. Leadership can only be effective within a specific context. Some people may think that Julius Caesar, Mother Teresa, Ronald Reagan and Bill Gates are all defined by being "great leaders" and that the traits they have in common define "leadership."

We beg to differ. Though it is always tempting, and sometimes insightful, to draw parallels between business leaders and religious, social, political or military leaders, such parallels are as likely to mislead as they are to inform. If leadership is described in such broad and all-inclusive terms, it risks being trivialized into the highest common factor, or being pressed to support whatever prejudice the writer is trying to "prove." In this world, hype rules, and Dilbert's opinion truly is as valid as anyone else's.

Is "leadership" academically respectable?

Some academic writers would not be amused by Dilbert. Psychologists and other specialists have sometimes tried to "annex" the territory of leadership. Though they usually do not say so explicitly, they imply that only trained psychologists or even clinical psychotherapists have any valid opinions about leadership.

Even worse, psychologists simplify the issues of leadership, claiming that their part of the puzzle – emotional awareness – is *the* key issue. While they are right that emotional awareness is *a* key issue, they don't account for how this emotional awareness relates in real time with power dynamics and with the need to make money.

Is leadership just about emotional issues?

This simplification can be patronizing, as it doesn't recognize some central realities of leadership – for instance, the constant negotiating that leaders have to do, or the realities of rank and privilege. Most psychologists we've observed who work with business see themselves as knights on white horses, coming to save the crass and materialistic world of business from itself. They do not acknowledge the dynamic, creative, innovative sides of building firms and creating wealth, never having experienced the fun and rewards implicit in the best rough-and-tumble games of business.

Are business psychologists on a power trip?

When psychologists are in their white coats and their consulting rooms, though they usually don't realize it, they occupy a position of power vis-à-vis their patients. Even when the patients are called clients and are business leaders, they are relatively helpless people seeking assistance from the experts in an area where they (the leaders) are all at sea, and about which they are often apprehensive. As long as they can confine the discussion to their power alley – the emotional dimension – the psychologists are powerful and happy.

In our leadership consulting practice, the biggest shock for the young psychologists whom we hire is when they are forced to confront their own power needs for the first time. When they work with our clients, the consultant tag is nowhere near as effective in maintaining an unequal power relationship as the white coat they used to wear.

Anyone who is to be successful in advising organizations on leadership needs to understand how their own emotional and especially *power* issues relate to those of the client – and how their own relationship with the client impacts on the organization. The psychologist working in business has to realize the odd demands of working with an individual in a commercial and organizational context. It is quite unlike the traditional one-to-one consultation. It is like a psychologist or doctor going into a patient's house and treating him or her while he is at the breakfast table with his or her spouse, with the kids running around and asking questions. The client in that context would need to be respected for their role as a mother or father as well as that of patient.

What most psychologists don't know

This is why psychologists often – we believe – fall into the trap of viewing leadership as a discrete area, divorced from its context. There is more to business leadership than a psychologist can know, unless he or she has been active as a follower and a leader in an enterprise.

This book is a guide to *business leadership* – which we see as an inter-disciplinary subject of roughly the same level of academic respectability as the fields of *business strategy* or *marketing*. In business, strategy, marketing or leadership are best illuminated by blending academic insights with observation of what works best in practice – and by fully understanding the commercial and power imperatives with which all leaders grapple daily.

Incidentally, business consultants almost always do the same with emotions as psychologists do with power and economics – they ignore them, they deny them. The answer lies in integrating the two disciplines. Yet how many strategy consultancies employ psychologists? How many leadership consultancies employ business strategists?

Is leadership a matter of theory or practice?

In business leadership as with other business subjects, there is a fascinating dialectic between theory and practice – though, as one wit has said, the difference between theory and practice is greater in practice than it is in theory.

Good theory is invaluable because it encapsulates and reconciles ideas and practice. Good theory enables us to cash in on oceans of experience. But in our view, the theory of business leadership – just like that of marketing and strategy – is pretty piecemeal, *ad hoc*, and incomplete.

Even as far as it goes, the theory is an interdisciplinary blend of psychology, economics, systems thinking, biology, anthropology, physics, chaos, and complexity. Though we read academic psychologists for their own peculiar blend of insights, a rounded view of business leadership has to include the rather different insights that come from personal experience of trying to lead a commercial organization.

Intuition rules OK

"Business thinking starts with an intuitive choice of assumptions. Its progress as analysis is intertwined with intuition. The final choice is always intuitive. Were that not true, all problems would be solved by mathematicians."

Bruce Henderson[1]

Leadership is no exception to Bruce Henderson's dictum that business decisions are fundamentally intuitive. Yet it is sensible to inform our intuition with the best possible concepts and theories, validated by repeated experience.

Is leadership always necessary?

No.

The need for leadership varies over time. When the goal is crystal clear, leadership is not necessary. Leadership is a transitional thing. It's about progress – the right kind of change that fits the market, the people, and the time.

The only problem is that you never know when leadership is necessary. Any particular company may need new leadership just when it least feels the need – for example, when it is being very successful.

Markets don't care whether any particular firm has the right leadership. If leadership is missing in one corporation, markets will find it in another. This is usually how markets evolve most powerfully and productively – not by evolution within firms, but between them.

Is leadership individual or collective?

Should there be one leader in an organization, or many? Should everyone be a leader?

In the real world of corporations, we nearly always hold one person *accountable* for leadership, that is, for seeing that it happens. The person accountable is nearly always the chief executive officer (CEO) or someone similarly described. It is a short hop to describing such a person as *"the leader."*

It does not have to be this way. Leadership is a function, an activity, a way of doing things – it is direction-pointing, mobilizing, enthusing – whatever is necessary to get the group or corporation from the current state to a future state. Anyone can exercise leadership sometimes, or to some degree. Indeed, it is very difficult for a smart and responsible executive *not* to exercise leadership at some stage. Any unit or organization can never have too many leaders. A leader is anyone who takes responsibility for making something different and better, or who successfully cajoles other people to do that.

> *Smart quotes*
>
> Leadership shared is leadership multiplied
>
> "No man will make a great leader who wants to do it all himself, or to get all the credit"
>
> Andrew Carnegie

Conversely, the full leadership role as described in many books – including this one – can seem at times superhuman. The leader must be mature, have superb people skills, display a complex intelligence, be both open-minded and flexible, as well as realistic and inventive. Only the most arrogant or deluded person would claim to have all these attributes.

It is nearly always better to have many leaders than one leader. There are many examples of leadership in crises coming from the most unlikely plac-

Q: Must the leader always be right, at least when making formal announcements?

A: Hell no. Most people in leadership positions have far too overdeveloped
an ego and therefore feel that they must always have an answer. It is infinitely better to be wrong, and seen to be wrong, than to persist in error.
A leader who acknowledges his or her mistakes can expect other people
to do the same.

es, from people who are not "meant" to be leaders. Everyone who has convincing ideas can and should become a leader.

Leadership in any unit or firm is not necessarily a full-time job. Different
people can exercise leadership at different times. Leadership is creating a
coherent and credible picture out of the mist of uncertainty, describing an
answer that is believable, and that is then believed – so that people do things
differently. Because different people will have different insights and experience, a group is likely to get to a better answer if leadership is a shared and
informal activity. Because people will be more effective in doing something
they believe in, and are more likely to believe in something that they have had
a hand in evolving, shared leadership is generally more effective.

Smart things
to say

Leadership is a culture, not a
person.

This is not to suggest that everyone in a firm should define
their own vision and strategy. What we mean is that as
many people as possible should be aware of what is happening and share their insights on what needs to change
and how this should be done. Such shared leadership
will not only enhance the robustness of decisions – having
harnessed many intelligent perspectives – but will also
promote successful implementation, by ensuring that people
feel part of the decision-making process.

Knowledge – clearly digested information – is to the organization what oxygen is to the body. Widely dispersed knowledge is fundamental to successful leadership. The speed and universality with which useful knowledge is shared determines corporate success. Newly interpreted knowledge is the only effective way of changing corporate behavior. The boundary between sharing new ideas and leadership is fuzzy and indeterminate. Everyone who attends forums for sharing and discussing leading ideas and forums for leadership should be sharing in leadership and encouraged to leverage their own leadership capabilities.

But shouldn't the chief executive also be the "chief leader?"

In some ways, it is expecting a lot to ask one person to be both the chief executive – the person who *does* things – and to be the "chief leader." Execution is about efficiency and pursuing an agreed direction. Leadership is about changing the direction. Execution is conformist. Leadership has to begin with heresy. Leadership is about being unreasonable, disruptive, experimental, and, dare we say it, *inefficient*. There is no efficient way of changing direction. If a radical enough change is necessary, its cost is irrelevant.

There is a kind of "Peter principle" about leadership. The Canadian educator Laurence J. Peter told us that "in an organization, each person rises to the level of his own incompetence."[2] Each executive gets promoted until he or she fails, through incompetence, to rise to the next level. The exception, possibly, is the chief executive. Since there is nowhere else to go, the CEO may or may not be incompetent; the fact that the CEO has not been promoted is not necessarily evidence of incompetence.

But with leadership, the chances are that the CEO *is* incompetent. Though some CEOs may rise through demonstrated leadership, most will get to their executive suites through skill at management, especially management of earnings. Skill at management is not necessarily incompatible with skill at leadership, but it is not a natural bedfellow.

Good management is primarily about efficient running of existing systems. Good leadership is primarily about tearing up existing systems in the quest for something radically different. Even if someone is naturally good at both management and leadership, the *urgent day-to-day role of good management is likely to drive out good leadership.*

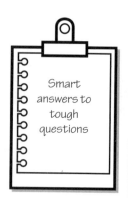

Smart
answers to
tough
questions

Q: Shouldn't leadership emerge from an organization's great unconscious? Why do we need leaders at all?

A: Leadership usually *does* emerge, to some degree, and that's great. And it's perfectly fine and dandy to have many, many leaders, and to have "roving leaders" who pass the baton back and forth. But the great unconscious usually works too murkily and too slowly to fit in with changes in the environment; still less to create them before some other enterprise does. Markets demand change. Change demands leaders. Organizations without leaders typically don't change until they have to, and then it's too late.

Surely the chief executive should be accountable for leadership?

It is much easier for a part-time chairman to be a good leader than for a chief executive, regardless of personality or skill at leadership. Sadly, the *role* of the CEO is to maintain, not to innovate. A chairman or an interested non-executive director is much more likely than the chief executive to spot the need for discontinuity, for a radical shift of gears, and much more likely to want to promote such a shift.

This is one reason, perhaps the most important (though rarely acknowledged as such), why both the American and British systems of corporate governance have, in their different ways, evolved a separation of roles at the top. Under the American system, the role of *chief operating officer* (COO) can be very valuable in making the CEO less biased towards execution and more open to innovation. If you don't have to run the show, it's easier to contemplate turning it upside down. In the UK, large companies often have a full-time chairman, whose responsibilities generally include "strategy" and long-term direction. The chairman's real role – though the Brits are too polite to say it, and often don't realize it – is leadership.

We would much prefer a corporate governance system that is more explicit than either the US or UK model. In our ideal world, each large corporation would have two positions at the top. One would be the "chief executive officer" (CEO), more colloquially the "chief executive." The other would be the "chief leading officer" (CLO), normally called the "chief leader."

Neither would report to the other; both would report to the board of directors. Neither would automatically be more senior or prestigious. In times of relative stability, the CEO would be the more important role. In turbulent times, the CLO would have greater influence on success or failure. The CEO and CLO would need to work effectively together, and might sometimes swap roles for a time.

Yet, at any one time, the difference in roles would be clear. The CLO's job description would be short: (1) to shift corporate direction when necessary, and (2) to maximize leadership skills throughout the corporation.

The chief leader needs to ensure that there is sufficient diversity of leadership for the firm to be prepared for any eventuality. At the same time, the chief leader needs to ensure that there is one common vision about the firm's identity and future; and that knowledge is properly shifted and integrated so that trade-offs and decisions are made relative to that vision. In this way, necessary and often painful changes can feel like progress to the whole organization.

OK, it's time to concede some ground. One person must be accountable for exerting and maximizing leadership. Organizations that leave leadership to chance sometimes thrive spectacularly, but much more often die young.

If there isn't a chief leading officer, and no other executive has explicit accountability for leadership, then the next best individual to be accountable for leadership is the chief executive. Clear accountability at the top, even if imperfectly bundled with other and often incompatible accountabilities, is better than none at all.

SMART PEOPLE
TO HAVE ON
YOUR SIDE

Warren Bennis (born 1925)

Bennis is the best-known, and probably the best, writer on leadership. A populist academic, born in New York but long tanned by living in southern California, and a writer on leadership since 1959, Bennis has aged gracefully. Only the snippiest of intellectuals have anything bad to say about him.

How can he help us? Well, we could read his excellent 1985 book[3] based on a study of 90 leaders, including a sports coach, an orchestra conductor, and astronaut Neil Armstrong. Not a bad idea, but here's an instant encapsulation of the key points. All 90 leaders, Bennis said, had four common attributes:

- *Management of attention.* This entails a snappy vision that "provides the all-important bridge from the present to the future." Leadership is "the capacity to create a compelling vision and translate it into action."
- *Management of meaning.* Communication to you and me. How does a leader do this? The leader must be trusted, and offer hope; but also be able to paint a vivid picture, coin a telling phrase, and master memorable metaphors.
- *Management of trust.* "The emotional glue that binds followers and leaders."
- *Management of self.* Bennis invented "emotional wisdom" long before "emotional intelligence" became all the rage. He meant the ability to accept people, warts and all; to live in the present moment; to treat everyone with respect; to risk trusting everyone; and to embrace failure and full self-knowledge. "The learning person looks forward to … mistakes." Leaders "simply don't think about failure, don't even use the word." Instead, real leaders bungle, make mistakes, or experience glitches.

Two other Bennis aphorisms are worth constant recall:

- "Leaders commit people to action, and convert followers into leaders."
- "Managers do things right. Leaders do the right things."

Bennis has done more than anyone to democratize leadership. He says that leaders are made and not born, that charisma and unusual skill are not necessary, that anyone can become a leader, and that leaders are necessary at all levels in business and society. For Bennis, leadership means harnessing peoples' constructive skills to make a better world.

His idealism is refreshing, though overdone. We don't believe that leadership is easy. While the top echelons should have no monopoly of leadership, and it would be wonderful if everyone became a leader, this isn't going to happen. The experiences necessary for significant leadership – unusual intelligence and emotional maturity, and the ability to belong and not belong simultaneously – mean that a minority of people will always have to supply a majority of leadership. We do agree with Bennis that to become a leader you must fully become yourself. But the reverse does not apply – if you fully become yourself, you do not automatically, or even usually, become a leader.

What makes a good leader?

We've already listed some of the specific skills needed by leaders but, deep down, what makes a good leader? What personality and expertise are ideal?

In our view there are five key and common attributes of good business leaders:

They must have the intelligence and confidence to handle complexity. They must be able to work out where to take a company. They must recognize business patterns and be able to assess evidence from many quarters – from customers, competitors, outside experts, and from people within the firm. Because business varies between industries and between firms, and because pattern recognition is the key to good business judgment,[4] most leaders are better at leading certain types of business than at leading others. We do not believe in "universal leaders," or in the type that can lead as successfully in politics as in business, if they can lead in business at all. If hiring for a leadership position, we would always hire a good leader proven in a similar business, rather than an excellent leader proven in a dissimilar business.

- Leaders must have the capacity to listen to others – and hear the subtext as well as the text.

- Leaders must be able to assert their view when they think they are right. Having weighed up all the evidence, they must take a firm line, even when in their own minds it is still a "51/49" decision.

- They must be perceived to have integrity, that is, to be able to describe things in ways that hang together. What they say and the way that they say it must have credibility and reflect a sincere view. Though there is a place for manipulation in business, those who are seen to be manipulative, cynical, or dishonest cannot function as effective leaders.

Of course, this means that the leader must be accepted by the group – which is often as much down to the group as to the individual. This is another reason why leadership is situational. A leader may be accepted by one group but rejected by another.

Ideally, leaders should be able to articulate vision and direction in an inspirational way, and live what they are talking about. The latter is actually more important than the former. Many great business leaders are introverts and some are not at all articulate – one of us can never forget the shock of hearing Richard Branson, who is clearly a great business leader, speak *ad lib*, to a friendly audience, and stumble over the simplest words and ideas. But if talking the talk eloquently is not absolutely essential, walking the walk sincerely is. For example, you cannot always persuade a consulting team to work late at night and at weekends unless you are willing to do the same.

Are leaders born or made?

Habitual leaders have certain ways of working, certain patterns of behavior, and certain assumptions about the world, that appear so deep-rooted and intrinsic to their personality as to suggest that they were always there, or, more likely, that they developed early in childhood. Early experiences probably give a minority of people the appetite for leadership.

Yet those experiences and that appetite are not what are commonly imagined. Leaders are generally *not* the kids ordering their peers around in the playground – the self-confident people with a natural air of authority are much more likely to become excellent managers than excellent leaders.

In contrast, leaders commonly experience a sense of separateness and even rejection early in life. In a curious blend of security and insecurity, leaders evolve a sense of their own worth by being aware of how tenuous acceptance is. They are aware that something is missing, so they are willing to try hard, and force themselves to be impressive. They take pride in accomplishments that they could never take for granted. Leaders grow to be able to handle being the lone voice, to be comfortable in isolation. Yet leaders do not wish to remain "lone wolves." They need to be connected to other people.

Leaders typically develop very strong "coping" mechanisms early on; the ability to deal with a hostile or threatening world. They learn how to resolve conflict, not just avoid it. They become strong because they know that they are weak. They attain identity and treasure it because they were never certain who they were or what they were worth.

Although they begin with uncertainty, threat, and rejection, leaders are the ones who make it through to a reasonable degree of security and acceptance. They have good experiences as well as bad, and the good ones tend to be more recent. Consequently, they are comfortable on the edge.

Leaders have usually experienced serious personal crises – yet come through them in one piece. Many people who start with the same bad experiences as leaders are never determined or lucky enough to break through to success. Perhaps through no fault of their own, they don't grow. Except through strange quirks of fate and extreme circumstances, they are unlikely to become effective leaders. Those who do not accept themselves, as well as question themselves, will never be accepted by others. Leadership requires the confidence to take risks, not through desperation or panic, but through the urge to explore – because previous exploration has sometimes led to great gratification.

Leaders learn to feel simultaneously insiders and outsiders. They must identify with their tribe, but not be "one of the boys." They must be self-aware and aware of the tribe and other tribes. There must always be a chink between the reality felt by the tribe and that seen by the leader. The leader has some lateral perspective. The leader must be willing both to defer to group prejudice and to manipulate around it; there is a creative edge that is determined to transcend the tribe's current limitations.

There really is no such thing as a natural leader, in the sense that leadership is like falling off a log. Leadership is not a spontaneous matter. It comes from blending intelligence, unusual perspectives, and a strongly developed

So you think you are a leader?

- What personal crises have you survived?
- Why do you think of yourself as an outsider as well as insider?
- What perspective do you have that your people don't?
- Why are you willing to confront anxieties that others avoid?
- Why are you insecure to this day?

sense of self and of other people – and from *wanting* to exert leadership, which implies a restless nature. Nobody who is totally happy with life can be a good leader. Nobody who does not believe in themselves can be a good leader. But equally, nobody devoid of self-doubt can be either.

Smart answers to tough questions

Q: What do I do if I'm the CEO and decide I'm not a good leader?

A: You can resign. But if you're good on other dimensions – for example a superb strategist or manager – you might want to consider other solutions. You might anyway. You could use a chairman or other executive or outsider as the main leader and defer to him or her on leadership issues. Or you could hire consultants who can fill the leadership vacuum – for as long as it exists. Probably the worst thing you could do is book yourself on a celebrated leadership course led by a world-class leadership guru. If you know you're not a good leader and could never become one, you know a lot more than most chief executives.

Are women better leaders?

We think so, though we can't prove it.[5] Both through observation and from theory, we believe that outsiders who break through to acceptance in the mainstream tend to become better leaders than those without a similar experience. Immigrants, women, Jews, and gay people are all examples. The common theme is "I haven't been brought up to lead, but I'm going to anyway."

Women and other outsiders are detached as well as attached. They center themselves to cope with their difference. Self-doubt grows into self-awareness, and is channeled into achievement. Outsiders become part of the tribe they lead, but never lose their separate identity. They have additional perspectives.

Women have to fight to get to the top. They have to get tougher. They must manipulate other people. They become self-aware. To be successful, they have to get a grip on themselves. They learn how to cope with exceptional stress. It is no wonder that those men who do not have similar experiences tend to be less good leaders.

Should leaders be gentle or tough, democratic or autocratic?

It depends.

It depends first on the leader's own personality. Leadership guru William Shakespeare made the point "to thine own self be true."

It depends next on the leader's colleagues. What are the skills, cultural expectations, and personalities of the other members of the leadership team, and of the organization at large? Different leadership norms reign amongst university faculty, oil rig workers, and investment bankers. There are also national and regional differences. What would seem simply good manners in Stockholm might appear tentative and confusing in Houston.

It also depends on the extent and speed of change necessary. If a firm is going bust, autocracy may be applauded. If a company needs to change direction totally, yet has a year to do so, and depends vitally on independent action by a large number of employees, widespread consultation and participation is advisable. Most valuable firms today comprise people who think for themselves and who do not check in their brains at reception.

Effective leaders are sensitive to colleagues' and customers' expectations, and have a repertoire of roles and behaviors. They can reinvent themselves from year to year and from minute to minute, as the environment requires, without losing their identity or integrity. Effective leaders also know the value of surprise. They are unpredictable without being arbitrary.

What is the opposite of leadership?

It is not "followership." Being a follower is a responsible position, with a wish to get things done. The opposite of leadership is lack of constructive engagement – apathy, indifference, or total detachment.

Leaders and followers are clearly symbiotic – they are necessary to each other, and they are attached to each other to mutual benefit. Without followers, there are no leaders.

Yet followers do not just follow; they often lead. The aspirations and frustrations of followers, as much as his or her own personal agenda, are what propel leaders to make changes. The most effective leaders often follow the undercurrent already well developed among followers, yet add the decisive leadership ingredient in the right place and at the right time. Followers in search of a leader are more likely to find what they want than a leader in search of followers.

There is another point. Leaders are there to multiply leadership. There is no vision, no destination, no purpose, no product, no business formula, no successful combination of forces, which is anything other than provisional. There is always a better way to do anything, and always something better to do. No one person is going to work it all out. Each leader should spawn masses of new leaders, each confident enough to create change, and anxious enough to want to.

Can leadership be learned?

If so much of leadership potential is developed early in life, what is the point of the leadership industry? Why, indeed, did we write this book? Why are you reading it?

Yes, leaders happen. But so too do smart students. This is not an argument against educating them further, or helping those whose job is to lead, to do so better.

Leadership and education are in fact very analogous. In both cases, the key is internal motivation, followed by focused and individual coaching. The very best results come from innate ability enhanced by individual learning and practice.

There is also a difference. In the case of leadership, the beginning of wisdom is self-awareness and the willingness to take responsibility, and to make responsibility and self-development grow together.

Though there can be personal development without leadership, there can be no leadership without conscious personal development. The real point about leadership is not what you know, or even what you do, but who you are. Yes, you must know or at least sense something others have not articulated. Yes, you must care enough to do something about it. Yet knowing and caring are not enough.

The *need* for leadership lies not in what should be done, nor in the desire to help others, nor even in the rewards from successful leadership. The *need* for leadership lies in the leader, in his or her need for self-expression through the medium of collective achievement. Without a deep-seated personal need of this nature, leadership either becomes a perfunctory job performed by rote, or simply too much trouble. Either way, there will be no memorable results.

Leadership and sainthood are incompatible. Leadership is about your own personal development. About not being a perfect person. About taking responsibility for your own development. The impulse for leadership and the mechanism to enhance it are very similar to the impulses and mechanisms behind Alcoholics Anonymous or any great religious movement. You strive because you are imperfect – yet you take charge of yourself.

In business, leadership is not altruism, and altruism is not leadership. If you are in business to make a fortune, you should not deny your greed. Anyone who is serious about business must want to make money for themselves, and an inevitable part of the same job is making money for close colleagues too. Great things happen more often through avarice than through goodwill.

Making money does not necessarily involve leadership. You could be a follower, or a one person business. But to make money *and be a leader* implies a willingness to take responsibility and develop yourself. It matters not whether the motives are base or selfless, whether your reward is in heaven or on earth. The way you evolve is the same. You have to start with yourself and your deep-rooted personal needs. You have to learn about yourself, about how you cope with the world, and about how you deal with others.

Is there one dominant way to become a better leader?

In much of the leadership literature – to pick on one case, in the work of Stephen Covey – we detect a prescriptive view. To exaggerate slightly, there is a path or program to follow: here are the paths or righteousness, or leadership, or whatever. "Follow this approach and you will become a great leader." There is little scope for ambiguity, experimentation, or uncertainty.

We too believe that some ways are more likely to succeed than others, and have no hesitation in saying what we think they are. But we cannot stress enough that when we see effective leaders, we know that they are not following a book or a set of rules imprinted on their personal organizer. And when we see leaders develop from being indifferent leaders to good ones, or from being good to being exceptional, it is not because they just went on a great leadership course.

What, then, is it? Is it because effective leaders have delved within themselves, and practiced the process of leadership? The process is one of emotional and rational intelligence – of appreciating and shaping external reality, both the complexity of people, and the complexity of everything else: ideas, things, economics. Effective leaders know who they are, and how this relates to the micro-world of business in which they operate – what they can see that others can't; what they and partners can do that nobody else is doing. Effective leaders love the process of immersing themselves in messy reality and shaping it, by getting other people to do what they would not otherwise have done.

Leadership is an art not a science, a process of building "leadership muscle" and "leadership agility." Leadership cannot be taught. Yet like all arts, leadership can be learnt.

If you want to be a leader, come with us on a voyage of self-exploration. We will supply the raw material gathered from other explorers, and from our own small expeditions. But you must paint the picture. If successful, you will end up not with a landscape of the promised land, nor a sketch of your tribe, but with a self-portrait, one stuffed full of imperfections, yet full of life and hope.

Notes

1   Bruce Henderson quotations in this book are taken from a series of *Perspectives on Strategy* issued by The Boston Consulting Group at various dates between 1973 and 1980. A useful collection of these and other *Perspectives* is published in Carl W. Stern and George Stalk Jr. (1998) *Perspectives on Strategy from The Boston Consulting Group*, John Wiley & Sons, New York.

2   Laurence J. Peter and Raymond Hull (1969) *The Peter Principle*, William Morrow & Co., New York.

3   Warren Bennis and Burt Nanus (1985) *Leaders: The Strategies for Taking Charge*, Harper & Row, New York.

4   In our view, business is "fractal" in the same way that leaves or clouds or coastlines are fractal – similar but different, with recognizable patterns repeated endlessly and variably. The rules of thumb that work well in one business may lead to disaster in another. The idea that business is fractal is derived from chaos theory. See Richard Koch (1997)

The 80/20 Principle: The Secret of Achieving More with Less, Nicholas Brealey, London/Currency Doubleday, New York, and also Richard Koch (2000) *The Power Laws of Business*, Nicholas Brealey, London. The US edition of the latter is Richard Koch (2001) *The Natural Laws of Business*, Currency Doubleday, New York.

5   In 1998, Gemini South Africa conducted a study of leaders and identified leaders who performed highly on all four of the "balanced score-card" quadrants. In our study there was a significantly higher proportion of women – but the numbers were low, and there is no guarantee that special South African conditions do not apply.

3
The Triangle of Tensions

"Knowing others is intelligence; knowing yourself is true wisdom. Mastering others is strength; mastering yourself is true power."

Lao Tsu

Leadership fantasies

Nineteenth century poet Emily Dickinson told us:

Success is counted sweetest
By those who ne'er succeed
To comprehend a nectar
Requires sorest need.

People commonly envy their leaders, seeing them enjoy much of what everyone aspires to – power and control, status, rank and privilege, and variety and stimulation in their work. After all, when you become a leader, all the drudgery, insecurity and need to push for recognition and reward recedes, and is replaced by a sense of "having arrived," with minions, money and outside expertise readily available to help do the job. And yes, there are bound to be tough times and demanding targets, but these seem a small price to pay – with the luxury of office and the prospect of a juicy pay-off even if you fail.

Moreover, leaders are the "superstars" of their organization, with people commonly "dreaming up" interesting information about their private, public and professional lives, often based on truth, but usually vastly exaggerated. Journalists, writers like Tom Peters, and in some cases business leaders themselves – Lee Iacocca and Richard Branson spring unaccountably to mind – create great larger-than-life legends. Business superstars possess acumen, foresight, authority, superb timing, negotiating and communication skills – they are perfect leaders, ideal grist to glossy celebrity magazines and bland TV chat shows. Admittedly, some of these leaders may avail themselves of the ego-serving spin of a good case-study writer "neatening and tidying" the story, exaggerating the role of the protagonist, and cropping luck and the less-than-ethical from the picture. How odd it is that, in time, most of these business heroes will fall from their perch – proving that getting rich and making a name for oneself are easier than true leadership.

Leadership realities

If we actually ask business leaders what it's really like, we hear a very different account. Most corporate leaders find themselves "torn" – many would say "mangled" – between being who they naturally are, being whom others want them to be, *and* managing the complexity and paradoxes of the here and now.

Smart quotes

In Chapter 1 we mentioned that leadership brings with it the essential, universal tensions of *yin* and *yang*. True, yet in order to understand the full reality in which leaders operate, it is more apt to represent a leader's dilemma as the "Triangle of Tensions" – a three-way conflict (Fig. 3.1).

The Triangle of Tensions depicts leaders struggling in three separate, but simultaneous, dimensions:

- *The Individual Identity* – who the leader really is.

- *The Canned Role* – the formal expectations, trappings and power of the leadership job.

- *The Emergent Process* – the messy reality; what is really happening within and around the company.

As the Greek letter Delta, the triangle also represents *change* – a fitting symbol for leadership, whose remit it is to move things from where they are to where they need to be. Primarily, however, the triangle implies tension

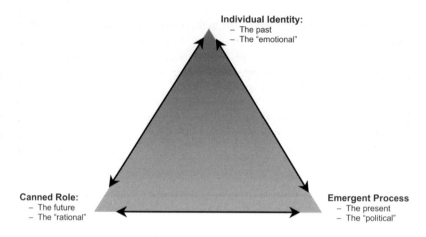

Figure 3.1 The Triangle of Tensions. © Yudelowitz, Koch & Field 2002.

– with each aspect (corner) promoting itself and detracting from the other two – explaining why leadership is so demanding and complex.

Let's explore each corner of the triangle – and see how *you* would cope.

The Individual Identity

This is who the leader is when he falls asleep at night and when he wakes up in the morning. His Individual Identity is rooted in the *past* and in his *emotions* – including his hopes, personal aspirations, anxieties, fears and prejudices. It is the engine of his motivation, and is therefore the source of his basic style of coping or managing in the world and at work.

The complexity of human personality is vast and is only partially understood. It is shaped by the interplay of many factors: genetic, social, cultural, and parental. All of these factors are important, and as with other mysteries of the universe and nature, discovery of *who we are* can never be complete; we are always work in progress. A few theories can help.

Games people play

Eric Berne's theory of transactional analysis provides a model that is especially useful to leaders, giving great insight into how our early life shapes the way we operate as adults. Berne describes how during early childhood, influenced by our parents, we develop certain values ("credo"), which forms our "script" in the world.

The script is a set of self-reinforcing assumptions that shape our interpretation of events, and response to them. The assumptions are at the core of our management style. The script is based on certain fundamental decisions (what Berne calls "injunctions") which the child takes to make sense of and deal with the world.

From the age of 6 to 12 the child learns to *cope* with the "big world" outside the home. The reality of this time is that the values that form the basis of his script are frequently violated. As a result, the child develops a coping or management style to restore, maintain and reinforce his belief system or assumptions, and so regain a sense of control and certainty in the world. This coping mechanism is based on his having learnt how to productively channel the energy evoked by the violation of his values ("script") into thoughts and behavior that he has ascertained (probably through trial and error) will restore his sense of how to be in the world.[1]

ERIC BERNE (1910–1970)

Originator of a major cognitive theory, author of best-selling books, skeptic, rebel, visionary, son of a writer and a medical doctor, a Montreal Jew who emigrated to California, three times divorcee, father of four, poker player, psychiatrist – Eric Berne was all of these.

Berne – whose original name was Bernstein – reinterpreted and updated Freud's concepts. For the first time, Berne's new framework, Transactional Analysis (TA), allowed unqualified people to apply the concepts, for their own and others' benefit.

Berne began as an academic psychiatrist and in 1947 wrote the outstanding – but difficult – work, *The Mind in Action*. The book comprised sound concepts of human nature and its relationship to the real world, and hence to the world of work.

In 1956, Berne's application for membership of the Psychoanalytical Institute was turned down. This rejection was a turning point. Berne reacted by dissociating himself from psychoanalysis and by developing TA.

Berne's new framework became famous through two excellent best-sellers:

His *Games People Play* (1964) was followed in 1967 by Thomas Harris' *I'm OK, You're OK*.[2] These texts have allowed lay people to make sense of themselves and take responsibility for their actions, making adult choices and decisions that transcend the traps of habitual behavior.

In *Games People Play*, Berne tells us that "the two most powerful urges of human beings are the creative urge and the destructive urge." At the core of his model is the complex notion that struggle and difficulty are linked to opportunity:

> *"Every wish that is gratified brings them closer to their goal, which is a feeling of peace and security, or freedom from anxiety ... No-one ever quite attains the goal, because new wishes are springing up all the time, and there are too many wishes trying for satisfaction at once ... Life is full of irritations like sour cigars and bitter women ... No wishes, no anxiety. A corpse never gets stage fright. People think they are looking for security, but what they are really looking for is a feeling of security, for actual security, of course, does not exist."*

Berne believed that each of us has a life script, or a way of being in the world, that is written early in childhood – beliefs like "I need to prove my worth," or "I can cope on my own." The script governs the way we see the world.

Yet – and this is his real value to us today – Berne showed how people can change. The script exists, and we need to understand and acknowledge it, yet we can rewrite it to gain more control and happiness. TA is anti-deterministic – people have choices. What has been decided can be "re-decided."

The final and most important lesson from Berne – one consistent throughout his career – is that responsibility for change lies with the individual, each individual.

For leaders, his message is clear – leaders, like everyone else, should beware of taking on too much responsibility on others' behalf, and beware too of trying to control personal change processes.

The leader should not do all the leading, but rather develop, spread and integrate the leadership of other people in the business.

Join the racket club

By the time we reach adulthood this coping mechanism becomes "hard wired" or embedded into a reflexive pattern – what Richard Erskine termed a "racket."

Why "racket?" It's like the Mob's racket. It's self-perpetuating. You pay the Mob to protect yourself, but it's a trap. The protection reinforces the threat. One gains short-term protection, but also reinforces the Mob's capacity and reason to force you to pay again and again.

The "racket" channels one's emotional energy and motivation into self-serving, self-reinforcing thought and behavior. Yet it operates like a subconscious program, which is trying to resolve past issues and traumas, rather than responding to the present, the here and now. Like a CD stuck on the same note, we are trapped into a few characteristic responses, regardless of what is called for.

Smart quotes

How rackets trap us

"If something hurts me, the hurts I suffered back then come back to me, and when I feel guilty, the feelings of guilt return; if I yearn for something today, or feel homesick, I feel the yearnings and homesickness from back then. The geological layers of our lives rest so tightly one on top of another that we always come up against earlier events in later ones, not as a matter that has been formed and pushed aside, but absolutely present and alive."

Bernard Schlink

Marion Milner, a psychoanalyst writing in the 1930s, described as "blind thought" what Erskine later called the "racket":

"It was only that my blind thought ["racket" – induced habit] had been reminded of the past by some chance likeness [trigger] and then behaved as if the present were the past."[3]

The "racket" operates as follows: day-to-day or momentous events (triggers) that violate our value system [script] evoke a familiar emotion (reaction), the energy of which is channeled into a *habitual* thought and behavioral *response*. This *response* will "set others up" to respond in a particular way – one that reinforces the trigger and therefore the pattern, restoring a sense of certainty and control. In so doing, the "racket" simultaneously promotes our interests and *traps* us in a *habit*.

The "script" and "racket" form the core of *all* leaders' management styles. They are therefore the part of the "Individual Identity" most relevant to his executive, organizational role. Typically speaking, his choice of career, the decisions he takes in his role, the way he takes them and how he characteristically relates to others, are largely driven by his reflexive behavior patterns (racket). Therefore, although he believes he is operating perfectly rationally – from choice – he is often just coping habitually. Most senior executives' "rackets" are highly adaptive to business and organizational life, being the source of their energy and motivation. In that way the racket is their greatest strength. Nevertheless, it's also their "Achilles' heel" because, rather than encourage deliberate choice, it is automatically evoked and, because it operates compulsively, will drive one's responses often without one knowing.

A racket, a habitual pattern of behavior, is not always dysfunctional. Many key leadership qualities – achievement orientation, tenacity and resilience in the face of adversity among them – may emanate from your racket. But if you have the invariant response to the same stimulus, it will only be coincidence if the response happens to be appropriate. Learning to control your racket means engaging in thoughtful and considered responses, in selecting the response *appropriate* to the real world, not the automatic one that gives you immediate comfort but which will probably just compound your problems.

You will become a much better leader if you gain *awareness* of your habitual patterns in all their permutations. You can then take responsibility

HOW FRED'S RACKET OPERATES

Fred is a successful CEO. His script tells him to achieve high standards. But his efforts to raise his firm's profits and stock market value fail.

This failure acts as a *trigger*. He feels anxious *(reacts)*, but instead of staying with the feeling and facing up to the reality of what he is experiencing (i.e. being confronted by failure), which would have promoted his personal growth and may have enabled him to get what he really needed, he channels the emotional energy into a behavioral *response* of working hard – on his own (because of his belief that it is important to be successful, he will tend to avoid asking others for help).

His colleagues see Fred as a self-starter, and, though he is the boss, his people impose higher standards on Fred, and leave him to sort out the company's dilemmas. (The chief financial officer, Randy, who hopes to get Fred's job, is not sure that the company's problems have any solution, until the market downswing ends. He is happy to leave Fred to carry the can.)

Being left in splendid isolation reinforces Fred's *scripted* assumption that he has to sort out the mess. Yet the weight of his own and his colleagues' expectations reinforces Fred's fear of failure and consequently his *racket*. Though he can see the firm's problems, Fred can't see how his behavior is just making things worse.

He thinks he is being rational, not compulsive, in buckling down alone. He doesn't know that he is coping to restore a sense of certainty and control, based on childhood injunctions (deep decisions) about how the world should be.

Only if Fred understood himself better would he realize that hard work is no substitute for leadership. He needs to call together all his *close* colleagues – and anyone else who can help – to work out a *realistic* new strategy, and to commit everyone, including Randy, to making the new strategy work.

for your racket and know when to invoke it, and when not, developing complementary responses. You can then act from *choice* rather than *habit*.

Q: I'm willing to buy your theory about rackets. I can see characteristic responses every time I push my colleague's buttons. But how do I find out what my own rackets are?

A: Three ways. First, introspection. Pause every time an important decision has to be made, and ask whether your response is habitual or versatile. Second, ask colleagues for their frank and unvarnished view (you may or may not get it). Third, find a coach or an objective diagnosis that will identify your rackets. (See note 4 for our recommendation.)

Smart answers to tough questions

HOW MARION CONQUERED HER RACKET[5]

"In the face of the hard facts of my own imperfection, it [Marion's racket] set one all sorts of impossible standards without my knowing it. It wanted me to be the best, cleverest, most beautiful creature and made me feel that if I was not all of these things then I was the extreme opposite, the dregs of creation and utterly lost.

"I found that [my racket's] judgments were hardly ever moderate. It liked either-or statements, wanting everything to be either good or bad ... I would find myself assuming perhaps that my work was very good and then plunging to the opposite attitude as soon as I came up against an inevitable fact showing me that it was not perfect. I would find myself swinging from attitudes of superiority to inferiority and back again with most disconcerting suddenness.

"I now began to understand why it was no good arguing against obsessive fears or worries, for the source of them was beyond the reach of reason and common sense ... They flourished in the no-man's land of mind where a thing could be both itself and something else at the same time, and the only way to deal with them was to stop all attempts to be reasonable and face up to them as they are."

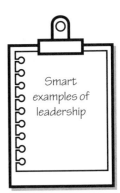

Smart examples of leadership

The Canned Role

Quite distinct from the Individual Identity is the "work role" or "Canned Role." This is the formal part of a leader's job and comprises the expectations others have of him or her, and all the trappings of rank and privilege.

Smart quotes

> A mask can unmask the truth
>
> "Man is least himself when he talks in his own person. Give him a mask and he will tell you the truth."
>
> Oscar Wilde

Whereas *Individual Identity* is primarily about the *past*, comprising our systems of meaning, value and emotion, the *Canned Role* is about what the organization is trying to achieve through the leaders' office – in this sense it is about the *future*. It's what the person who holds the leader's job is meant to be and do – the formal job description, prescribed objectives, targets, duties and responsibilities. The Canned Role includes the boundaries of the leader's authority, linked to codes, policies, procedures and organizational charts.

Why "Canned Role?" Because it's like canned laughter on a television sitcom. It's not spontaneous. You get it on demand, and it's always predictable.

Consequently, the incumbent is "set-up" by others to perform in a particular way, with rights and duties carefully prescribed regardless of the leader's personality or views. The more organized and professional an organization, the more careful and thought-through its design and processes, then the less able the leader is to shape his own role. This is the classic trap of "Organiza-tion Man," a trap even more severe for the boss than for the subordinate.

SMART EXAMPLES OF CANNED ROLES

"In the average company, the boys in the mailroom, the president, the vice-presidents, and the girls in the steno pool have three things in common: they are docile, they are bored, and they are dull. Trapped in the pigeon-holes of organization charts, they've been made slaves to the rules of private and public hierarchies that run mindlessly on and on."

Robert Townsend[6]

"No question, now, what had happened to the faces of the pigs. The crea-tures outside looked from pig to man, and from man to pig, and from pig to man again; but already it was impossible to tell which was which."

George Orwell[7]

Smart things to know about leadership

In his Canned Role the leader is caught between a rock and a hard place. Subordinates expect the leader to provide direction and certainty. The or-ganization, the financial analysts and the media all expect superior world-liness, technical know-how, and charisma; for him or her to show the way, make things safe, and get things moving; to reassure that someone's in the cockpit flying the plane. But the same people, especially subordinates, also demand to be involved; to be able to have their input and opinion acknowl-edged and heard; to be recognized for their experience and knowledge. They want direction, yet if the leader acts decisively, they will complain.

Whilst employees require that their bosses see beyond appearance and stereotype and judge them for who they really are, they grant their leaders no such latitude.

Still, the Canned Role is not without its pluses. Knowing what is expected can be liberating. Paradoxically, it can create the security necessary to move beyond fixed boundaries – to experiment, to deal with the ambiguous, messy realities of enterprise.

- Do you use your Canned Role automatically or deliberately? Consistently or selectively? Do you generally disregard it and "act yourself?" Or do you generally play the role and disregard your own idiosyncrasies?
- Has the power of your Canned Role increased or decreased? Has the way you have used the Canned Role been partly responsible for this?

The Canned Role provides the leader with *license,* by virtue of the fact that it accords significant status and influence. For instance, one telephone call from a Fortune 500 CEO may open up otherwise closed doors. Also, the Canned Role provides the leader with substantial opening credibility and power. Used with *awareness* and *perspective,* deliberately and selectively, the Canned Role can be invaluable. Yet the Canned Role is squandered, devalued, and abused if used to shield the leader from reality or in pursuit of privilege. Most dangerous of all is when the Canned Role induces a CEO to believe the propaganda turned out by his press office or the public relations advisers.

Smart quotes

<u>Sell hubris</u>

"When a CEO's picture appears on the cover of *Fortune* magazine, it's time to sell the shares."

IMD Professor Paul Streoble

The Emergent Process

Besides the rational intent of the Canned Role, and the patterns of emotion, meaning, motivation and behavior of their Individual Identity, leaders have to cope in a third sphere: the here and now, the *Emergent Process*.

In the Emergent Process, interests converge or clash, compromises are struck, decisions taken, and reality unfolds. This dimension is where the self-interest of the individual – derived from the past – and the future-oriented Canned Role come together, and clash also with chance events, to make things happen. The Emergent Process provides loose and spontaneous *yin* to mitigate the formality and tight definition of the *yang*-oriented Canned Role.

The Emergent Process is influenced by a myriad of factors – intentional and unintentional, explicit and unobservable, physical and conceptual, human and technological, small and large, negotiated and chance – all of which collide to create change.

Five arenas are useful, both to describe Emergent Processes, and to give the leader a handle on them:

- *Pattern recognition* – how to recognize what is happening.

- *Negotiation and power* – how to exert personal influence.

- *Rhetoric and framing* – how to describe the new reality.

- *Timing* – how to intervene when events will favor you.

- *Physical proximity* – how to be center stage.

Pattern recognition

Chaos and complexity theory tells us that most events occur because of non-linear feedback systems. Reality is a result of a multitude of variables interacting. At any time, only a few of these variables will be at all important. The problem is that we cannot predict which few variables will count. Precise links between cause and effect are impossible to unravel. In a word much used by the theorists, events *emerge* – and therefore outcomes are usually surprises.

Bad news for leaders? Not entirely. Leaders can learn to recognize how *patterns* are shaping, how order is emerging (as it typically does) out of the chaos. Where others see only disorder, those who understand something about chaos, and/or those who are experienced in working in a particular area and who have good instincts, can detect beautiful and fascinating patterns. Business leaders who know nothing at all about chaos or complexity sometimes do this marvelously well. They may not know what they are doing, they may not even be able to describe it coherently, but somehow their experience and intuition, derived from long immersion in a particular market, enables them to sense how to act when everyone around them is confused and paralyzed.

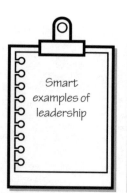

Smart examples of leadership

THE NATURE OF CHAOS AND COMPLEXITY

"Tucked away between stability (what is known i.e. has happened) and instability (the uncertain future i.e. what will happen), at the frontier (i.e. what is happening: the emergent boundary between the present and the future), non-linear feedback systems generate forms of behaviour that are neither stable nor unstable, but emerge in discernable, yet continually evolving patterns."

David Parker and Ralph Stacey

Understanding the nature of chaos and complexity is well worthwhile for leaders and indeed for anyone who wants to make money in business. We can provide only the briefest description here.[8]

We can infer potential outcomes based on patterns of behavior we notice, and act accordingly. But as we can't predict the consequences of our actions, we have to learn as we go along, and then decide our next actions. The future *emerges*.

Negotiation and power

The leaders' role here is managing "the moment" and being essentially political. It involves timing and the ability to appreciate an opportunity when it presents itself: to scheme, and skillfully use language to influence others and get things moving.

This process is almost always controversial. Arnold Mindell, the originator of *Process Oriented Psychology*, postulates that all social or human progress is preceded by conflict, either interpersonal or intrapersonal. The leader must be comfortable with power, conflict and negotiation.

The political dimension of leadership is often dismissed or suppressed. It ruins the flow of inspirational books. Too bad. The manipulation of power is critical to acting on and shaping our environment and getting things done. Total alignment and harmony, or too much humility and tolerance on the part of the leader, may stop an enterprise adapting to new conditions.

KILLER QUESTIONS

Are you comfortable using power and confronting conflict?

To use power, you have to negotiate with others. Effective leaders negotiate all the time. Other leaders, well qualified on most dimensions, shy away from negotiation. This reticence is doubly misplaced. Negotiation is necessary to exert power responsibly and institute change that would not happen otherwise. And, contrary to popular belief, people like "being negotiated." Employees like the clarity and choice that negotiation gives. "If you do this, then you can have that." "OK, boss, but if I do this and that, I would prefer to have this and the other." "Done."

Rhetoric and framing

Rhetoric or purposeful language is one of the most effective tools in applying one's power and getting things done and for getting organizations moving in a particular way.

Organizational myths, legends and sagas are other essential tools. Use them lavishly, and ensure that they drive home the particular spin that will energize your cause.

Framing means the way information is presented, the spin that is put on it. If something good happens, the truth is that many people and other forces *may* have been responsible. Yet praising the type of behavior you want, praising an individual exhibiting such behavior, and attributing the result to that behavior, is a shrewd way of reinforcing what you want. The same goes for blame, though be careful, publicly, to stigmatize only actions, not people.

Frame things simply, to get the change you want. If possible, frame things first. Respond immediately to major triumphs or disasters, putting the spin on events that will motivate the right actions.

Timing

"Strike while the iron is hot." In business, especially in large organizations, the iron is usually lukewarm, or totally cold. Pick your moment with extreme care. Only try to influence people when a decision is imminent.

JACK WELCH'S USE OF RHETORIC

Jack Welch, the former CEO of GE, is especially skilled in the use of rhetoric in persuading others to accept and act on his view of the world. He uses stories, maxims, myths, analogies and slogans to make action happen. These rhetorical devices, especially when they are emphasized and consolidated with well-timed decisions and public appearances, or public censure, are critical to implementing strategy.

Smart examples of leadership

The 1990 GE Annual Report supplies an example of Welch's word-painting:

"We have been pulling the dandelions of bureaucracy for a decade, but they don't come up easily and they'll be back next week if you don't keep after them. Yes, we've taken out lots of structure – staff, spanbreakers, planners, checkers, approvers – and yet we have by no means removed them all. Those who have cleaned out an attic and returned a year later are often shocked to see that what they've left as "essential" – the pairs of old pants that would never be worn for painting that would never be done, the boxes of old mouldy *National Geographics* that would never again be read. I feel the same way every time we visit our management system – our processes – and see the barriers that insulate us from each other and from the only reason for existence as an institution – serving customers and winning in the marketplace"

Welch tells another graphic story:

"I had a technician at my house to install some appliances recently. He said, 'I saw your video-tape on Work-Out. The guys at my level understand what you're talking about: we'll be free to enjoy our work more, not just do more work, and do more work on our own. But do you know how our supervisors interpret it? They pointed to the screen and "you see what he's saying. You guys better start busting your butts."' We have a long way to go."

Physical proximity

When Henry Kissinger was appointed to the White House he made sure that he was assigned an office close to the president's. This physical proximity enables influence through frequent informal interaction. As Henry says, physical nearness "counts for much: the opportunity to confer with the President several times a day is often of decisive importance, much more than the chairmanship of committees or the right to present options ... it may be as simple as the psychological reassurance conferred by proximity just down the hall."[9]

Smart quotes

Match proposals to the moment

"Finding the right set of circumstances to advance one's ideas is critical.
A good idea at the wrong time ... will be ignored and shunted aside.
On the other hand, an idea for a new product that would otherwise have languished may be received eagerly if times are tough, the competition keen, and attention focussed on promising new products."

Jeffrey Pfeffer

KILLER QUESTIONS

Are you close enough to the seat of power?

An opposite case was when General Motors' chief financial officer Rob Smith tried to introduce strategic planning to the organization. The planners chose a basement location to emphasize confidentiality. The opponents of strategic planning used this with relish to ridicule "the boys in the basement." Fortunately for General Motors, Smith's planners never exerted mainstream influence.[10]

Holding the tension – the state of personal mastery

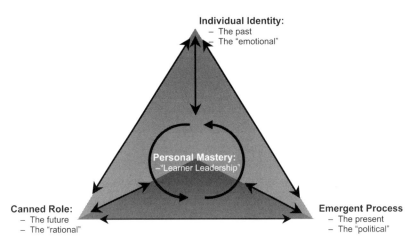

Figure 3.2 Holding the Tension © Yudelowitz, Koch & Field 2002

Although each aspect of leadership – *Individual Identity*, the *Canned Role*, and the *Emergent Process* – is critical, it is destructive if one dimension is consistently emphasized at the others' expense. Hence the *art* of leadership involves holding the tension between the three points of the triangle: the *emotional, rational* and *political*, or put another way, the *past, present* and *future*. Holding the tension does *not* mean occupying the middle point between these aspects of leadership so as to *compromise* between the three. Rather, good leaders recognize that the dynamics, imperatives and pressures of each dimension are different.

Leaders must have the wisdom to judge which of the three "corners" needs to be emphasized at any one time and to understand the impact of the decision on the other two dimensions. The leader needs to see *all* sides and to distinguish the inevitable from that which can be influenced through judicious intervention.

Deploying the Canned Role selectively

Business leaders enjoy and make the most of the rank and privilege of the "Canned Role," *but* at the same time, use them selectively, prudently and reliably – for the good of the cause, rather than the good of the leader. They appreciate the impact and cachet that rank can have; yet have a detached and philosophical approach to the adulation and status that can come with being a leader, understanding that much of how others see one is based on fantasy, and that leaders can go from hero to zero in the twinkling of an analyst's eye.

Swimming through uncertainty, reaching the shore

Winning leaders realize that the future is complexly determined and that linear paths are illusory; that it is difficult to sort signals from noise – yet still act decisively, pursuing goals resolutely, even as the goals and the goalposts slide into different games. The leader's job is to absorb uncertainty, to shield their people from most of it, yet take the new information, make sense of it, and realign the enterprise accordingly – all while not breaking stride or losing a smile.

Leaders have the courage to see things as they are, as opposed to how they want them to be. Leaders appreciate the emotional, political and rational

Smart quotes

Progress requires heresy

"Progress depends on the toleration of unexpected [thought] and behaviour and heresy is essential to the welfare of a community. A nation that does not permit heresy will remain stagnant."

George Bernard Shaw

elements of experience – and extract the essential value from different, often unpopular, ideas.

Self-awareness

Personal mastery is ultimately about self-awareness. It is a long trek, for every individual, to become clear about who we are, and who we are not.

Owing to human complexity, self-awareness can never be complete; we are works-in-progress, and our self-awareness always lags behind our evolution. Self-mastery implies accepting one's strengths and weaknesses, the positive and good side of one's personality as well as the negative or shadow side. It involves having a clear perspective on one's assumptions about the world and how one naturally strives to reinforce these – and maintain a sense of control and certainty. It therefore entails being aware of one's personality and how this impacts on one's relationships within organizations and society.

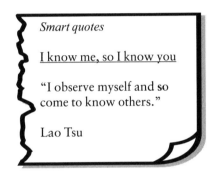

Smart quotes

<u>I know me, so I know you</u>

"I observe myself and so come to know others."

Lao Tsu

In particular, self-mastery means realizing how our rackets, our default self-reinforcing coping patterns, affect our work – how they drive us on, yet trip us up. Rackets compulsively and unconsciously reinforce our assumptions and values – stopping us seeing things for what they are.

The ancient Chinese sage Lao Tsu noted that much of our power is wasted in maintaining our assumptions and beliefs, defending them and foisting them on other people. We forfeit our power to change, by using our power to stay the same.

Lao Tsu also observed that people who lack self-acceptance and insight, lack personal power and feel fear. Tyrants, for instance, exert power over others, yet feel frustrated and impotent rather than powerful. If we lack self-awareness, we tend to spot evidence in others' behavior of what we cannot accept in ourselves, and believe that we are more right than we are.

Personal mastery, in contrast, implies self-acceptance. It means taking responsibility for our "script" and "racket" (how the world impacts on us, and how we impact on the world), forgiving but not excusing our short-comings. It's about being mindful of our imperfections so that we can deal with them.

Personal mastery needs to be supported by a particular style and process of leadership: what we call "learner leadership." Through learner leadership, the "chief leader" ensures the development of an effective leadership culture throughout the enterprise. Leadership culture leverages the strengths of every individual, transfers information and relevant knowledge and attitudes speedily throughout the organization, manages complexity and paradox – and creates wealth now, tomorrow, and, with luck, for a long time to come.

It is to learner leadership that we turn next.

Notes

1 This account is based on the excellent and under-appreciated work of Richard Erskine. See Richard G. Erskine (1991) Transference and Transactions: Critique from an Intrapsychic and Integrative Perspective, *Transactional Analysis Journal* 21, 63–76.

2 Eric Berne (1964) *Games People Play*, Grove, New York; and Thomas A. Harris (1967) *I'm OK, You're OK*, Harper & Row, New York.

3 Marion Milner (1934) *A Life of One's Own*. Chatto & Windus, London.

4 For an excellent and inexpensive diagnosis, we recommend using the Life Path Insight ("Lifepi") method, which can be done totally confidentially via the Web: go to www.lifepi.com or email info@lifepi.com. Readers should note that two of the authors have an indirect financial interest in Lifepi.

5 Marion Milner – see note 3 above.

6 Robert Townsend (1970) *Up the Organization*, Michael Joseph, London.

7 George Orwell (1946) *Animal Farm*, Harcourt Brace Jovanovich, New York.

8 Readers are strongly advised to read further about chaos and complexity. The best short accounts that bring out the business aspects are: David Parker and Ralph Stacey (1994) *Chaos, Management and Economics*, Institute of Economic Affairs, London, and Chapter 9 of Richard Koch (2000) *The Power Laws of Business*, Nicholas Brealey, London, or the US edition, Richard Koch (2001) *The Natural Laws of Business*, Currency Doubleday, New York. The best single book about chaos is still James Gleik (1987) *Chaos*, Little, Brown, New York (also available in a Penguin paperback). This classic book is highly accessible and exciting, though business readers may find it a trifle long-winded.

9 Henry Kissinger (1979) *The White House Years*, Little, Brown, Boston.

10 This example is taken from the excellent book by Jeffrey Pfeffer (1992) *Managing with Power: Politics and Influence in Organizations*, Harvard Business School Press, Boston.

4

Learner Leadership

"It is the best possible time to be alive, when almost everything you thought you knew is wrong"

Tom Stoppard, *Arcadia*

The irony of learning to lead

A friend of ours is fond of saying, "When I want to learn about a subject, I write a book about it." Once, frustrated by the guide books to Venice, which all focused on the main tourist areas, he wrote a walking guide to the city's back streets. Leadership is very much like that. To teach, you have to learn. To learn, you have to sense what you don't know, and be *prepared* to learn. Your Canned Role may be that of the master, but you are also an apprentice. You learn and you teach as you go along.

Once you are aware of, and to some extent managing, your triangle of tensions, it's time to *practice* the art of leadership. *Practice* means not just doing, but rehearsing, studying, training, exercising – just as a pianist practices. Practicing implies a blend of confidence and humility. There would be no point spending a couple of hours a day practicing the piano if you weren't going to give a good performance; but equally, you need to practice hard if the performance is to be any good.

There is an added dimension to leadership. Not only must you learn, practice, and lead, but you must simultaneously teach others to lead, and stimulate leadership as widely as possible among the people you influence. In learning and doing, you have to teach as well. You teach by example but also more directly – by involving your people in the leadership process, and even by articulating what you are all doing as you do it. It is as though the concert pianist gives lessons at the same time as practicing and performing.

How can a leader do all this?

Sounds tricky, doesn't it? Fear not – it can be done. And think of how much time you're saving. If you can learn and lead and multiply leadership all at the same time, you're doing three valuable things at once.

The process of learner leadership is not easy, yet it can be described and remembered easily. It is shown in Fig. 4.1 – the Wheel of Learner Leadership.

Smart illustrations of leadership

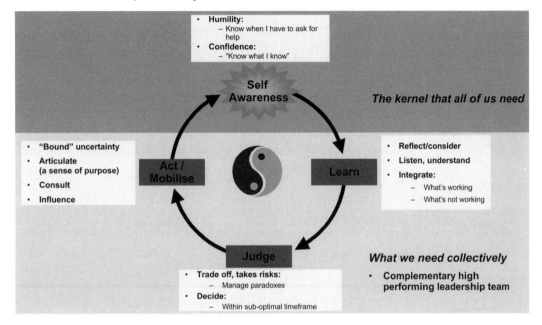

Figure 4.1 The Wheel of Learner Leadership © Yudelowitz, Koch & Field 2002

The Wheel of Learner Leadership

Round the circumference of the wheel, we see that there are four stages to leadership:

- self-awareness;

- learning;

- judging; and

- acting and mobilizing.

These are sequential stages, yet each stage depends on success in the previous stage. It is also a wheel, because life and business are one long and seamless process where each stage comes round time and again.

Within the wheel, is the Taoist symbol for *yin* and *yang* – listening and telling, inspiring and driving, coaching and doing, supporting and demanding. The leader must continually oscillate between soft and hard, between the emotional and the rational, even between love and results.

Let's scrutinize each of the four stages of the wheel, and learn some techniques to increase effectiveness in each.

Self-awareness

Self-awareness is the cornerstone of learning to lead.

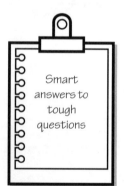

Smart
answers to
tough
questions

> Q: What, precisely, do you mean by "self-awareness?"
>
> A: Two things. It is knowing who you are, knowing who you are not, and knowing the difference between the two. And it is the process by which learner leadership – of everyone in the organization – is achieved and constantly renewed.

Scottish poet Robbie Burns (1759–1796) reflected on the value and difficulty of "seeing ourselves as others see us." Self-awareness could scarcely be better defined. Between 1905 and 1931 we learned from Albert Einstein, Niels Bohr, Werner Heisenberg and Kurt Gödel that there is no objective reality in the universe. People are no exception. There is no objective "you." This does not mean that there is no useful perception of you, or that every person's opinion is of equal (and low) value. What is interesting is *"inter-*

subjectivity" – how you are generally perceived within any group or situation. That is the closest that we can get to the real you.

For leadership, it is vital that you understand how you are seen by others in as many contexts as you operate in. "Others" is not a single or homogeneous group. There are many "others." For some you may appear an ideal leader. Other individuals would not follow you if you could show them a quick and open side entrance to heaven.

Self-awareness also has two additional elements. There is a hidden component, of which you are aware and nobody else, or few others, are aware – yet. Say you are a tennis champion and enter the tournament at Club Med. Or that you are afraid of snakes but your colleagues have never before been with you to the snake-infested outback.

There is also a technical component – what you know, and what you don't. Of course, it is impossible to know exactly what you don't know. You have to sense it, and be sensitive to it. Most people underestimate the gaps in their knowledge. The appropriate response is not to mug up an encyclopedia. It is to use experts for purposes that you tightly define, and to keep checking that the knowledge they are giving is relevant for your decision.

But by far the most important dimension of self-awareness is what others make of you – the response that you elicit just by being who you are (whom you are perceived to be), and by specific actions you take in each context.

Smart things to say about leadership

"Having an IQ in the top 1–2% of the population is a drawback when it comes to leadership. You need to be smart, but not a genius. The smarter you are, the more you need to work on your self-awareness."

Being self-aware is extremely difficult. It is not correlated with conventional intelligence. Many highly intelligent people have very poor self-awareness. They are too caught up in intricate and complex mind games to notice what people with lower IQs are thinking.

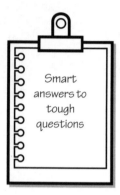

Smart
answers to
tough
questions

Q: It's all very well telling us that self-awareness is vital, and then that it's difficult. That's not very helpful. The real question is: how do I improve my self-awareness?

A: Excellent point. There are three ways that any reader can start to use now, and there is a fourth, additional way that is more time-consuming and expensive, yet more complete. The first two ways have to do with *feedback* and the third with *embarrassment*.

First, the simplest, easiest and most universal answer is to always *be open to feedback*. Ask for it honestly, openly, and in a spirit of self-doubt. A *genuine* spirit of self-doubt. One of us once had a boss who was a great leader in many ways, but who was lacking in real self-awareness. He would constantly ask, "Am I right?" or "Am I wrong?" But most of the time he didn't want an honest answer. The answer he wanted was that he was right. He could become quite aggressive if told he was wrong. Few people followed this route. Therefore, as one of us once told him, "the chairman is always right." Don't be like the chairman. Encourage an honest answer. Pay more attention to your respondent's eyes than her mouth. Listen for the hesitation, the unspoken contradiction. Watch the body language. Make yourself vulnerable. And be prepared for the answer to hurt. It's often best to ask for feedback when you are in an "up" mood, and can cope with some bad news.

Second, *organize the feedback process*. Get someone else to organize the feedback process. Make it *multi-sourced* and *multifaceted*. Multi-sourced means asking several people. Not too many – they must be people who know you well, not people who only see your best side. They must be people you trust – there is no point in asking for an opinion you won't respect. Ideally, choose three subordinates, two peers, and your boss. If you don't have a boss, choose someone as close to this role as possible. Multifaceted means that the exercise should ask a lot of quick questions about how you are seen in many different contexts. The process must be *anonymous*. You must not know who said what (though you may have your suspicions …). All that is reported is that three people said this, two people said that, and one didn't know. That sort of thing. The questions must be quick and simple to respond to, and people should give their first answers without revision. Don't go in for false quantification – a one to five scale, or whatever, is *not* recommended. Answers should be yes, no, or don't know. In the box on page 85, we give you our executive Leadership Style Questionnaire (the "LSQ"), a modified version of one we have used successfully thousands of times. Ideally, the process should not be one for the leader alone. All senior executives should go through the same process at the same time.

When you have the results, remember that *there is no objective reality, only inter-subjectivity*. There is no right answer. Therefore, the answers you are given cannot be wrong either. They just are. They summarize the impressions you are giving. Yet you shouldn't take the results at face value. Ask yourself, what *do* they mean? And, much more important still, *what are you going to do about it?*

The third way to develop self-awareness is through *embarrassment*. There's no learning without it. Embarrassment is one of the most uncomfortable emotions for any adult. Yet being exposed to embarrassment, and sticking with it for a while – not moving off into our self-preserving, self-serving racket – is a key to learning. Embarrassment is the process through which we face up to, and finally accept, the lessons that come through failure. The process can be described as follows:

Information > Denial > Confusion > PAIN > Acceptance.

Allowing embarrassment and pain to operate is to be self-aware. When we lack self-awareness, the confusion triggers our racket, so we remain un-self-aware and don't learn from experience and failure. Whole professions – including accounting and PR and large branches of management consulting – are designed to help top executives avoid embarrassment. Nevertheless, leadership demands embarrassment.

Valuable as these exercises and insights are, they are not really enough to develop a high level of self-awareness. For this, you need a framework within which to understand yourself and the perceptions others have of you. So our fourth and most important answer is this – you need to go through an outside process or program or exercise that is based on a useful psychological model, to learn to face up to yourself and the impression you make on others.

There are many, many such programs. The best way to select one is by personal, enthusiastic referral from someone whom you think of as "similar" in temperament and experience and seniority to yourself, someone whose judgment you trust. They must say, "I was somewhat skeptical before, but it really helped me, and I think it will help you." And you must believe him or her.

Still, let us tell you of three programs that we recommend for senior executives. One is the Recess College, which is an Anglo-Dutch initiative.[1] Another is the Center for Creative Leadership based in Virginia.[2] Courses usually take between one and two weeks and the fees are usually between $4–5,000, excluding travel and accommodation. A third, unique option is the "Lifepi" (Life Path Insight) Web-based initiative. No, don't laugh. It is based on a technique that has been successfully used, based on face-to-face interviews by qualified psychologists, for over 22 years by such organizations as the British Army, the National Health Service (in Britain), the Church of England, GlaxoSmithKline, and Dow. The Web-based version has three advantages. It is non-intrusive – you do not need to see or talk to anyone at all. It is relatively quick: it takes only about three hours. And it is relatively inexpensive, costing around $1000, or less if a large number of people are involved.[3]

THE LEADERSHIP STYLE QUESTIONNAIRE

Some sample questions

Please answer the questionnaire in two steps:

- Step 1 – positive characteristics: place an "x" next to items that particularly characterize the leader.
- Step 2 – suggestions for improvement: place an "o" next to items where you think the leader needs to improve.

If you have insufficient information, or no opinion, or the point is irrelevant, or the leader is neither particularly strong nor weak, leave the space blank.

1 Good investigator, analyst, and observer.
2 Good at passing information on, explaining things, and presenting.
3 Good at numbers, financial data, and interpreting charts and budgets.
4 Action person, determined, sorts things out.
5 Sees the big picture, creative, visionary, entrepreneurial.
6 Ambitious, shows initiative, tenacious, high energy, good under pressure.
7 Good to work with, open, co-operative, constructive, builds bridges.
8 Persuasive, influential, articulate, accessible, brings out the best in people and teams.
9 Good listener, willing to change his or her mind, accepts criticism, shares.
10 Handles stress, good negotiator, honest, independent, resilient.
11 Good at organizing people and projects, consults, follows up.
12 Good at using own time, sets priorities, effective, seldom panics.
13 Hires the right people, good coach, patient, willing to use "oddballs."
14 Respected professional, expert, innovative, asks for help when needed.

Smart leadership tools

Learning

Learning is the process of discovery – gathering facts and insights about what is going on, what's working and what's not, as a prelude to making important decisions. Without self-awareness, learning is likely to be too filtered; however, learning is a separate, discrete stage in learner leadership.

Learning is not an academic thing, nor necessarily conceptual. Learning implies the ability to sense and listen to what's going on around you and around the business. It is rational, yet it is *even more* intuitive. It is about business issues, yet it is also about people as individuals – employees, partners, customers, competitors.

The learning phase is when everything is debated, and options are widened as broadly as possible, without reaching closure or judgment. Learning in this context is specific to a particular decision about to be made, but specific to nothing else.

Learning must now be a collective process. Even if the leader is an expert in the area under consideration, now is the time to solicit and listen to input from everyone. As a leader who is learning, you must suspend your own

<u>Learning is exploration</u>

"We can no longer act as patrons, waiting expectantly for the right solutions. We are each required to go down to the dock and begin our individual journeys. The seas need to be crowded with explorers, each of us looking for our answers … In this new world, you and I have to make it up as we go along, not because we lack expertise or planning skills, but because that is the nature of reality. Reality changes shape and meaning as we're in it. It is constantly new. We are required to be there, as active participants. It can't happen without us, and nobody can do it for us."

Margaret J. Wheatley

Smart quotes

"Learning is appreciating what is *really* going on, not what we *want* or think *should* be going on. Learning means understanding when something *isn't* working, and saying so, regardless of how our ego and reputation are affected."

Smart things to say about leadership

<u>Learning is together</u>

"How will we navigate these times? The answer is, together … We need each other to test out ideas, to share what we're learning, to help us see it in new ways, to listen to our stories … We have each other's curiosity, wisdom, and courage."

Margaret J. Wheatley

Smart quotes

assumptions and hold your verdict back. Of course, you can only suspend your assumptions – or do anything else with them – if you know what they are. Hence we come back to the centrality of self-awareness.

In learning, open-mindedness, flexibility, and enquiry are the three most important attributes. The answer is *not* the point; at this stage the point is what's going on, and developing options for possible action.

When a decision is particularly important, or difficult, or controversial, and especially if it is all three, good leaders develop scenarios, generating as many different options and ideas as possible. They neutralize their own censors, putting them on hold. They seek advice from all quarters. They talk not, neither do they decide. They listen.

The listening leader has a secret weapon. Whether formally or in everyday interactions within a group, the leader uses a discovery technique that we call "Pass to the Right."

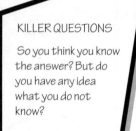

KILLER QUESTIONS

So you think you know the answer? But do you have any idea what you do not know?

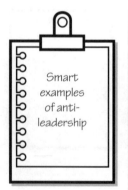

Smart examples of anti-leadership

WHY BRILLIANT INTELLECTS OFTEN BLOCK LEARNING

Brilliant academics and CEOs with brains the size of planets often share one thing in common which is totally destructive of learning and leadership alike.

They are not mature or humble enough to hear what they didn't know or understand before. They know that they are much cleverer than everyone else, so they don't listen to anybody else. They engage in trivial conflict with people who challenge the precise formulation of wisdom that they espouse. They have well-founded views; others' views are necessarily less robust.

Those who know, know. Those who don't, listen. Sooner or later, those who listen know more than those who know most.

PASS TO THE RIGHT[4]

"Pass to the Right" is a simple but highly effective discovery technique that ensures that everyone you want to involve in the process has their say.

Gather the people together and then explain the rules. You define the issue for debate and discussion. Then you start with one person who is allowed to speak for as long as he or she wants. Nobody is allowed to interrupt (except the facilitator, if there is one, who may intervene to clarify an issue or give process comments). When the first person has finished, he or she "passes to the right," to the person sitting on the immediate right, who then has his or her turn.

The process continues until everyone has had their say. The leader is last to speak. The leader's role is to listen, write, distil, and, when his or her turn comes to speak, to answer each person in their own terms, and then, only then, to give his or her own opinion.

It is a great technique for the still, small voice, often silent or ignored in groups where the loudest and most confident people monopolize the air-waves. It is also great for making disagreement controlled and calm. If you vehemently disagree with the speaker, you cannot shut them up. You must wait your turn. Knowing this, you calm down. You know you'll get to say your piece. Instead of generating heat, you prepare your intervention – you know that you will need to actively tell, and you manage that opportunity to your best advantage.

You are encouraged to speak personally, from the heart, "from the I," about how you feel about the issue and the situation. No one listens much to abstract views. You are also directed to give examples to put what you are saying into context.

The premise of "Pass to the Right" is that everybody has some wisdom, a piece of the puzzle. The problem is that organizations don't know how to gather all this information from around the table.

Smart leadership tools

The leader must respond and acknowledge each person's viewpoint. The leader must summarize it to the satisfaction of the person concerned, to show that it has been understood and taken on board – though it may not be agreed with. People are not stupid or unrealistic. They know they may have to give up their viewpoint. They don't necessarily want to win the day. If they are to lose the issue, they must first know that they've been listened to and that their perspective has been respected and acknowledged.

This is not a touchy-feely, all-things-to-all-people way of muddying the waters. It is perfectly OK for the leader or anyone else to say, "I hear what you say, you said x, but x is a pile of do-do. This is why." The only requirement is that you play back x accurately, to its proponent's satisfaction.

"Pass to the Right" is just one of the techniques a leader should use to gather facts and views on any important decision. The search is for grains of truth that can then be integrated, turning raw data into information, and information into useful knowledge. The more the leader is not an expert in a particular area, or feels that the facts are not properly appreciated, the more important to involve other people and extend the discovery process.

If the issue is controversial, do not be too linear or quick in closing off the discourse. A stifled debate will come back to bite you. It will resurface just when things are going badly and when your leadership is under most attack. If a discussion cycles round three times, with people repeating incompatible positions, this is an indication that fresh perspectives and data are needed. They may actually be there, under the surface, being expressed by body language and not words. There's probably a grievance that is not being expressed. At any rate, you know that people are not ready to go forward.

Do *not* say, "We're going round in circles, let's cut this off and move on." It may be wise to take a break, but not to move to a decision. Artificial closure is a negation of learning, and tolerable only on truly trivial matters that should not have been part of a discovery process in the first place. People hate to be cut off. It is better not to consult in the first place than to force closure when it is palpably premature.

Smart leadership tools

DEEP DEMOCRACY[5]

Democracy often means going with the majority, the 51% or so, or with the people with the most power, and assuming that the 49% have changed their minds because they were outvoted. But the 49% haven't been convinced. All that has happened is that they've been shut up. They are in opposition, and may emerge as terrorists or saboteurs.

Deep Democracy is a process used for very important decisions where there is serious divergence of views. Deep Democracy ensures that the 49% have their wisdom heard and perhaps incorporated into the decision.

Deep Democracy cannot be practiced properly on a "do-it-yourself" basis. It is grounded in quantum physics and Jungian psychology and requires a highly professional facilitator.

Deep Democracy uncovers as many points of view in the room as can possibly exist – more viewpoints than people, since individuals can hold multiple and contradictory views. These are probed for, using neuro-linguistic programming to become aware of all communication going on, putting non-verbal cues into words, and amplifying dissent and divergence.

A view may be an emotion or an opinion or an indisputable fact. It may be a rationally articulate and reasonable view, or it may simply be fear, devotion to an outmoded idea, or anger that is preventing someone from "letting go." Note also that a view is greater than an individual, and the individual is greater than the view.

Deep Democracy is suitable for mature and constructive teams, ones that are able to bear conflict and are willing to confront what they were unaware of, and would prefer to remain unaware of.

In Deep Democracy, the leadership role shifts and swirls, on the edge of chaos. Anyone could be the "Archimedes" who suddenly "gets it," who suddenly sees what should happen next. The leader's job is not to arrive at the answer, but to ensure that somehow it emerges.

Facilitation involves spreading that role amongst others. The paradox is that a view can only be heard if somebody "owns" and personalizes it. For instance, if I say it's important to have trust in this organization, people will switch off – it sounds abstract and pious. Yet if I say, "I don't trust you, because you promised me your support on the bonuses, but in the meeting on Wednesday evening you let me down, and I feel hurt and angry," and then someone else comes up with a similar story, maybe about another executive who's let them down, then everyone will understand the issue of trust in the firm. Once we really understand an issue and its meaning for real people, then we can take decisions and focus energy constructively.

Though Deep Democracy needs expensive facilitation and takes a lot of time, you can use some of the principles of Deep Democracy in less elaborate ways and in any context. Bring out the "no" view, the quiet view, the unpopular view, the suppressed view, the inconvenient view. Understand its personal context and why it holds power for its adherents. Do not paper over the cracks.

Try to get at the unexpressed grumble, the suppressed doubts, the latent conflict. Ultimately, it's OK for the leader to overrule anyone, but wise leaders ask questions like, "What would it take for you to go along with this decision?" "What do you feel most strongly about?" "What is the basic point that you feel hasn't been properly heard?"

In learning, good leaders are continually roaming around, searching for disagreement and ambivalence, and making colleagues aware of it. Why? Two reasons. One, it brings out the little fragment of wisdom that otherwise would get lost, so it helps to make better decisions. And two, it helps in implementing. Being heard respectfully, and being free to dissent, makes it easier to go along with a contrary decision and help to make it work.

THE TRUTH AND RECONCILIATION COMMISSION (TRC) IN SOUTH AFRICA

After the peaceful transition in 1994 from white minority rule to democracy in South Africa, President Mandela and the newly elected parliament decided to establish the Orwellian-sounding Truth and Reconciliation Commission (TRC), chaired by Archbishop Desmond Tutu.

The TRC's remit was to investigate all the alleged human rights violations of the previous regime. Anyone could make allegations and these were fully investigated. Everyone could tell their story and have it heard, without editing or compression. The TRC had the power to make any citizen give evidence and the power to publish evidence and its findings in full, but not to punish wrongdoers. Those who confessed to the TRC were granted amnesty for their crimes.

The background to the TRC was that, for many ordinary people within the ANC (the black liberation movement that became the governing party), and for a minority of black people generally, it was not enough to have moved to a non-racial democracy. An angry minority wanted to put guilty whites, or perhaps all whites, in re-education camps, send them into exile, or execute them.

The TRC produced a multitude of harrowing tales. The public, including many whites that had been unaware of the extent and horrors of the oppression, heard for the first time the human stories behind apartheid. The TRC did not deal in statistics. We did not learn that 35,000 people had disappeared.

Smart examples of leadership

Instead, we heard an old woman's account of how her son had been taken from her in the dead of night, and how she had struggled to find him or gather fragments of news about his death. We heard graphic testimony of torture, from both the tortured and the torturers. We listened to how individuals had suffered, how they had lost their reason, how specific people had fought to regain personal dignity, to exercise hatred, or to overcome it.

The TRC worked. It averted bloodshed. It gave the enraged minority a hearing, and belated respect from almost all quarters. It made the white minority pause for thought. The TRC was Deep Democracy at its best.

SMART PEOPLE
TO HAVE ON
YOUR SIDE

EDWARD DE BONO

Originally a lecturer in medicine, de Bono has evolved into a "thinker about thinking." His most famous and valuable concept is *"lateral thinking."* Unlike traditional "vertical" thinking, lateral thinking is non-linear, breaking out of established patterns in order to look at things in a different and non-continuous way. Lateral thinking leaps off in unlikely directions, using analogy and word association to turn conventional wisdom upside down.

In our terms, lateral thinking is useful in the learning phase, not in the next stage of judging. Lateral thinking cannot help make decisions; it just enlarges the range of options to be considered.[6]

One de Bono technique we can recommend for occasional use in learning is his *"Six Thinking Hats."*[7] Choose one or more individuals to assume particular mental approaches to an issue – each person dons an imaginary colored hat:

White = information
Red = feeling and intuition
Black = caution

Yellow = benefits
Green = creative thinking
Blue = structuring and organization of thinking
Just by assuming the role, individuals are likely to see more options. The roles should be rotated on different issues and at different times.

De Bono's work is useful for one dimension of learning – stretching and discovering what we know. It is not a complete solution. Remember that you also need technical knowledge, and to put your own censors on hold so that you can appreciate genuinely new perspectives.

Judging

Judging is making the decision, deciding what to do. Learning is concerned with effectiveness and opening up choices. Judging is about efficiency, making decisions in time, and shutting down options so that only one is selected. In learning, the leader appears to take a back seat. In judging, the leader drives.

Judging is risky as well as lonely. The leader cannot afford to prolong the learning stage too long. The data will never become crystal clear and unambiguous – except by draconian simplification. Judging nearly always means taking a risk on imperfect information and making a call under pressure of time. Time and knowledge are wonderful things, but you will never have enough of either. Judging is in tension with learning.

Smart things
to say about leadership

"Managers defer decisions.
Leaders take them."

You must trust your judgment and feel OK about the decision and reasonably comfortable with the residual uncertainty and ambiguity. Judging is not easy, nor is everyone good at it. The ability to judge separates the sheep from the goats, the action-oriented business person from the hand-wringing academic.

You may think the decision is finely judged – 51% on one side and 49% on the other – or, frankly, sometimes it seems like 50–50. We know some excellent leaders who have privately tossed a coin to decide, not from indifference or whimsy, but because any decision was better than no decision, and the evidence did not favor one course or the other. Having made the decision, you must appear confident and relaxed in communicating it to your associates, concealing your own doubts and vacillations.

KILLER
QUESTIONS

- Leaders always have a bias towards *either* learning *or* judging. What is your bias?
- What are you going to do to counter this bias?

Judging always makes trade-offs and is never wholly satisfactory. You have to integrate divergent points of view in a way that is good enough. Making trade-offs cheerfully and well is an art. It's about knowing when enough learning is enough. Learning is the *yin*; judging is the *yang*. Judging is the place for being decisive, where hard business reality – difficult customers, demanding owners, predatory competitors – intrudes and demands to be heard. This is also where astute leaders will *invoke* specific examples of "nasty" reality, to explain why it is time to judge and to do, and why the luxury of learning must be temporarily suspended.

Acting and mobilizing

Acting and mobilizing is the last stage on the Wheel of Leader Learnership. It's the action phase, when new directions are implemented. To get action you must communicate, act yourself, and mobilize others to act in the new way.

Yet effective acting and mobilizing depends on strong self-awareness, sufficient learning, and good judging. This is where it becomes highly personal to the leader. Getting people to change what they are doing, to follow novel paths, to escape the well-ordered ruts of the past and the present – what a job! Why should people take any notice? It's easier to give lip-service to the new concept and carry on doing what has always been done, and what, given the lag in reward systems, is probably still being rewarded.

Launching a new crusade

This is the test of a leader's powers of persuasion. And it is not primarily a matter of charisma. Charisma can be dangerous, if you turn it on unthinkingly. Charisma can also wear out. Once you have deployed charisma several times, people get inoculated against it. It's just the leader weaving his spell again. Pass the sick bucket, Alice.

Slick presentations won't help. Staying up all night to craft the address to the troops is daft. Employing a speech writer or communications expert is worse. You really can over-prepare. If you look at the issues again too carefully, doubts will surface, and intricate details will mesmerize. Doubts and details, banish them all.

What matters are two things. One is the process to date – the self-awareness, the learning, the judging. You can do nothing about that now. Either you've done a good job or you haven't. Just as when you were a student and you walked into the examination hall, it's too late now. You just have to do your best. What a relief! All that preparation is over. The other thing that matters is integrity. Do you believe what you are going to say? Do you believe it is important to the future of your people? Are you excited by the change ahead?

People are funny. We don't listen to an important announcement and give the speaker marks out of ten for logic, foresight, relevance, and artistic impression. We don't even think, initially at least, of how the change will affect us materially. We think whether we *believe* it. Is it important? Is it right? Does it stir our emotions?

People won't commit unless they believe you. The leader needs integrity if he or she is to be believed.

Offer blood, toil, tears, and sweat

"The high sentiments always win in the end, the leaders who offer blood, toil, tears and sweat always get more out of their followers than those who offer safety and a good time. When it comes to the pinch, human beings are heroic."

George Orwell

This is where integrity and the leader as a person are make or break. Each person in the audience will listen to the leader, to the way she talks, the way she moves, the feelings she throws off, oh, and yes, lastly, least importantly, to the words she uses – and each individual will either believe her or they won't. It's as simple as that. And whatever you or anyone else does afterwards, you can't overturn that individual, personal, simple, binary, immediate, visceral response. Check the box. The leader is right. The leader is wrong. Over. Sorted.

That is why you must be clear on how and why you took the decision and what it means to you, personally and emotionally. Why you must not say anything that you do not believe. Why you must be excited – quietly or volubly, according to your true personality. Why you must excite each individual, infecting them with your enthusiasm. Why you must display integrity – which is not just honesty, but wholeness. You and your cause must fit together, an entire and consistent package, offered up in total sincerity, powered by your dreams and your people's opportunity.

If you cannot communicate this, communicate nothing. Make no changes, or let someone else lead them.

In order to complete the Wheel of Learner Leadership, the leader must be acutely aware of how his or her communication is being received. Whilst telling, the leader must also be listening and observing. In this interplay, the leader's self-awareness becomes enhanced.

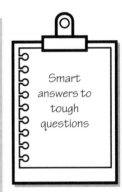

Smart answers to tough questions

Q: Why do all organizations suffer from a "communication problem?" Is the problem communications or something deeper? What can leaders do about it?

A: It is the individuals who suffer, not the organizations. The people suffer both from communication problems and from issues where this is just the symptom.

The communication problem is real. It is because *everyone* suffers from incomplete information. This is not a matter of details or parts, but of the whole. Where are we going? Why? How does what I do relate to something important? No one, not even the leader, can know all the answers; not fully.

There are also poor communications because everyone cannot be keyed into all information that *is* available. This is not primarily a technical matter, nor even one of intent and goodwill. It is a matter of numbers, diversity and power. If there are lots of people, especially people who are diverse and cannot easily pick up the signals from more connected people, then some people will know a lot more than others. If there are lots of junior people, beyond a certain point the value of communication will be exceeded by its cost. Sad, but true.

So "poor communications" is often a symptom too – a feeling people have that they are powerless and unimportant. That is the real problem, and to a degree, it is insoluble because it is true.

What can the leader do?

First, make the organization smaller. Divide it into tribes, if possible into autonomous tribes, maybe even tribes that comprise a new organization. Tribes communicate naturally. Tribes are like-minded groups of up to 150 people. Tribes operate best at around 50 or fewer.

Second, show a vision of what the "whole" is or what it could be. We don't need more information. We need more integral information – less, but more powerful, information; the hidden backbone that links together disparate masses of apparent reality. We need meaning. We need purpose. Create it. Bang on about it.

Third, realize that the chief leader is also the chief communicator; and that just as leaders should maximize leadership from everyone else, so too with communication. Like God and Big Brother, you will need to seem omnipresent. Move around and be visible everywhere, communicate crisply and with genuine passion the few things that really matter, and transfer the Holy Grail to everyone you meet – pass it on!

Fourth, inculcate a feeling throughout the organization that every employee is part of the whole; that they are on the team, that they have individual dignity and importance. If you can't honestly do this, outsource the functions currently performed by "unimportant" employees. There should be no such animal. If there is, it may cost you dearly.

Finally, be honest and open, to the limit of what is commercially and personally sensible. If you cannot tell someone the answer to their question, do not lie or fudge the issue. Do not give non-answers; people know when they are being fobbed off, and they don't like it. Simply say, "I'm sorry, I can't tell you that right now. I have to respect someone else's confidence and

> dignity (or whatever is the constraint on telling the full truth). I can't tell you *that*, but I can tell you *this*. Is that good enough for the moment?"

Every time you communicate something that you do not truly believe and live, you devalue the coinage of your leadership. Every time you excite because of integrity, you revalue your coinage. Think about it.

> • If your leadership was quoted on a stock exchange, would you stand near your all-time high, or near your low? What recent actions have lowered or raised your quote? What of the months ahead?

KILLER QUESTIONS

Permanent revolution, permanent communication, permanent action

Communicating a new course is not a one-off event. The new cause must be constantly reiterated, exemplified, celebrated, and driven forward in innovative ways. In doing so, the new cause itself will evolve into something different.

> JACK WELCH
>
> CEO of GE from 1980 to 2001, spectacularly successful and hugely hyped, Jack Welch still has something to tell the smart leader. Normally we would steer clear of the celebrated hero, partly because it has already been done and overdone (and how!), and partly because the feet of clay will inevitably emerge over time. The market is cruel, and the market is surely set for a correction in Jack Welch's stock.

SMART PEOPLE TO HAVE ON YOUR SIDE

But whatever happens next, Welch's record as a leader is extraordinary for this reason. He has taken a huge and successful bureaucracy, and turned it into an even more successful business, where individuals are important and allowed to create vast dollops of new value. Were it not an oxymoron, we would say he has created an entrepreneurial organization.

How this happened, and the extent to which it is really true, must lie beyond our scope. But here we note the means, because every leader can copy them.

First, and often forgotten, he trimmed the organization. "Neutron Jack" got rid of a huge number of underperforming businesses and people. Some naïve writers assume that somewhere along the way the "nasty" Welch turned into the semi-cuddly one profiled today. Yet without the cuts, and its simplification, GE could never have moved from being hierarchical to being more informal. Do not ignore this lesson for your own company.

Second, he allowed front-line workers, in tightly controlled and Jack-approved circumstances, to challenge their bosses and throw off unnecessary bureaucratic constraints. The process was dubbed "Work-Out," and was organized through GE's powerful Crotonville training center, a sort of cross between a university and a re-education camp. Welch was the sponsor and promoter of Crotonville, and seemed to be present, in person or in spirit, at all its conversion sessions.

Third, he promoted a series of "causes" to encapsulate the cultural change he wanted. From standards of excellence for customers, to "boundaryless-ness," to whatever new crusade-of-the-year he preached, Welch set out his stall and ensured that everyone listened. Those who followed his message, and who created new value, were amply rewarded – he changed GE's bureaucratic and undifferentiated salaries and bonuses to ones where the super-performers could get rich. "Boundaryless behavior is a way of life here," Welch reported. "People really do take ideas from A to B. And if you take an idea and share it, you are rewarded." "Middle managers," he warned, "have to see their roles as a combination of teacher, cheerleader, and liberator, not controller."

Welch talked about "inverting the pyramid," by which he meant that the focus should not be not on bosses but on front-line employees working with customers and business partners.

Finally, Welch was a one-man super-catalyst, madly dashing about from here to there, constantly finding and cross-fertilizing powerful new ideas from one part of GE to other parts. It is said that when he left one site, its executives are instantly on the phone to the next one, asking, "What exactly is this new idea of yours that Jack likes so much?"

Can you match Jack for evangelistic zeal, peripatetic energy, and promotion of local successes? If you fall well short, that is great news. You have bags of room to make your leadership much more mighty.

The mechanics of mobilizing

Just six hints:

1   *Delegate clearly*. Leadership should not be immune from boring but essential management principles. If you are not to do something personally, delegate the task to someone who is then accountable. Be very clear on who is to do what. If you ask two people to work on the same thing, ensure that they have clear areas of responsibility and are fully aware of what each other is doing. Impose deadlines, even if they sometimes have to be a bit fuzzy and need review.

2   *Whenever you use words, use actions too*. A cheerleader, a promoter, a boss, a preacher – fine. But be a doer too. Do some important things yourself. Make a difference, and everyone will notice. Make a difference on the things that are central to your cause.

3   *Create early successes.* Pay disproportionate attention to creating early victories, in line with the new direction. Conduct many experiments: some will work. Praise and publicize these early successes, and the individuals who make them work.

4   *Use power and remove those who do not co-operate.* Change management means changing management. If people will not change, they must be changed.

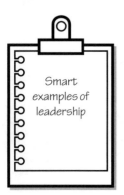

Smart examples of leadership

FIRING NON-CO-OPERATORS

"In one company, two of the leading barons [who resisted the new direction] were asked to leave. At a management conference shortly afterwards, the chief executive made it clear that they had been removed because they were isolationists; they were not co-operating. Ten years later the story is still told in hushed confidential tones."

Richard Koch, *Moses on Leadership*[5]

5   *Multiply leaders.* Find more and more people who are able and willing to lead in the new direction – not just to follow, but to initiate, and to encourage. These new leaders can then influence and start other people as leaders … in a chain reaction.

6   *Tell stories.* Jack Welch is famous for using myths and legends to get his point across. Many of the most effective leaders we know – and very few of the people we know who are more effective as managers than as leaders – use the same technique. Stories make the issue come alive. Stories are memorable. Stories are effective.

On to some other stories …

To prove the point, our next chapter is devoted to stories – based around three fairy stories. Proceed only when you are sitting comfortably ...

Notes

1   The Recess College in the UK provides excellent short "sabbaticals" for senior executives and is built around a ten day "College Block." The college is run separately for men and women since "each sex processes issues of power, influence and identity differently." The College is run by Elisabeth Henderson who trained at the Tavistock Institute, and founded Recess College in 1988. Call Elisabeth Henderson on +44 20 7792 3234 or fax +44 20 7792 2543.

2   The Center for Creative Leadership (CCL) in the US is a not-for-profit educational institution that trains over 27 000 managers each year. See www.ccl.org.

3   Go to www.lifepi.com or email info@lifepi.com. Readers should note that two of the three authors are indirectly financially interested in lifepi.

4   *Pass to the Right* is based on the methodology developed by Dr I. Adizes of the Adizes Institute, Santa Monica, California. See Adizes, I. (1992) *Mastering Change*, Adizes Institute Publications, Santa Monica.

5   *Deep Democracy* is based on Process Oriented Psychology and in particular the splendid work of Dr Arnold Mindell. See Arnold Mindell (1992) *The Leader as Martial Artist*, HarperCollins, New York.

6   Edward de Bono (1971) *Lateral Thinking for Management*, McGraw-Hill, Maidenhead, England. Also available in Penguin paperback.

7   Edward de Bono (1985) *Six Thinking Hats*, Penguin, London.

8   Richard Koch (1999) *Moses on Leadership, Or, Why Everyone is a Leader*, Capstone, Oxford.

5
Three Fairy Stories

"The fairy story that succeeds is in fact not a work of fiction at all. It is a transcription of life into highly simplified symbols; and when it succeeds in its literary purpose, it leaves us with a deep indefinable feeling of truth"

C. M. Woodhouse

Did you know that George Orwell gave *Animal Farm* a subtitle: *A Fairy Story*?

It's apt. Fairy stories operate in a world beyond morality. They reveal truth. As C. M. Woodhouse says, the message of all great fairy stories is: "Life is like that – take it or leave it."[1] Even if we wish to rebel against the truth, we must first understand its power.

This is a terrific and neglected lesson for leaders. The world as we find it is not hunky-dory. It is full of strange and amoral forces. And the stronger our commitment to making the world a better place, the more important it is to understand the rules by which the universe operates. Fairy stories can help us to do this.

Here are three fairy stories, and some further (true) stories about leaders that are related to the fairy stories. However good your memories of being a toddler, read our version of the fairy story first. There are many variants of the stories and we have adjusted a few details to make our point plain.

After reading each story, try to guess what point it's illustrating about leadership. It could be fun to do this with a friend or colleague, or as a team exercise. Perhaps your point will be as valid as ours, or even better (if so, please let us know!). Trying to guess the leadership implication will make both that and the story more memorable and therefore more useful to you.

SMART FAIRY STORIES

RUMPELSTILTSKIN

Based on the story by Jacob and Wilhelm Grimm.

Once upon a time, there was a miller. He was poor and had a habit of saying the wrong thing. One day he met the King, and, stuck for something to say, he foolishly boasted, "My daughter can spin straw into gold."

"This I must see," the King exclaimed. "Fetch her at once!"

The King was delighted to see that the miller's daughter was beautiful. He put her in a small room with a spinning wheel and loads of straw, telling her, "Spin me some gold by breakfast, or you'll die."

Well, of course, she had no idea how. She started crying. Suddenly, a weird little green man flew through the door. "I can help you," he said, "Give me your necklace, and I'll spin you some gold."

And do you know, he was as good as his word! In the morning, the King found the miller's daughter with three reels of golden thread.

"Excellent," said the King. "Amazing! But can you do it twice? Here's some more straw. Do the same thing tonight."

The miller's daughter was scared. But the peculiar little green man pranced through the door again. "I'll spin some more gold," he said, "if you'll give me the ring from your finger."

Before breakfast, the King was delighted to see the golden girl with the golden thread. "If you can make gold a third time," the King promised, "I'll make you my Queen."

Now, the King wasn't bad looking, and he was very rich. How proud my dad would be, thought the miller's daughter, if I became Queen. But when the strange green man reappeared, she realised she had nothing left to give him.

"Don't worry, dear," the little man told her, "if you become Queen, you can give me your first child in exchange for this lot of gold now."

The miller's daughter agreed, and that was how she ended up as Queen. She and the King had great sex, and before long a baby boy too. They were all very happy, especially the miller, who sold his story to *The Peasant's Gazette*.

The Queen had quite forgotten about the funny little green man, until one stormy night he reappeared. "I've come for your baby boy," he said. The Queen was distraught. "Take all my jewels instead," she begged. But the little man insisted on the boy.

"In three nights' time, I'll take the baby ... unless you can discover the secret code word."

The Queen and her counsel tried to think of every code known to the kingdom, but when she repeated them all to the little green man the following night, he just laughed. "No, no, that's not the code," he chortled again and again.

On the second day, the Queen asked her wisest adviser what to do. "Perhaps the code is a name," he said. "Let's get the census records, and then you can reel off all the names tonight."

So when the little green man came that night, the Queen tried all the names. "No, wrong again, ha ha," he kept repeating.

The following morning saw the Queen and the wise old adviser closeted together. "Don't despair," he told her, "perhaps it's *his* name. It's pretty obvious, I know, but he wouldn't be down on the census as he's just moved into the woods beside the kingdom."

So the wise old adviser set off for the woods, where he heard the little man dancing and singing,

"The Queen will never win my game,
For Rumpelstiltskin is my name."

When the little green man materialized that night, the Queen toyed with him.

"Is the code Twinkletoes?" she enquired.

"Nope! Wrong again!"

"Is the code Shagribanda, perhaps?"

"Getting desperate, huh," he guffawed. "Now one last guess, and then the baby please."

"OK. Is the code Rumpelstiltskin?" she asked, permitting herself a demure smile.

"Grrr!" exclaimed the little green man, stamping his foot with such furious force that he made a hole in the floor, and disappeared down through it.

And, strange to say, no one has ever seen him from that day to this.

If you want to work out the leadership implication, do so now, before reading the next story.

TRANSYLVANIAN GAS CORPORATION (TGS)

TGS is our disguise for a real client. In December, TGS's chief executive (CEO) presented a major investment program to its board of directors. Three of the four independent, outside directors took exception to the plan, claiming it was too much money and that there would be industry overcapacity soon.

When it was clear which way the wind was blowing, the two other executive directors on the main board – the chief operating officer (COO) and chief finance officer (CFO) – decided to play politics and cover their backs, distancing themselves from the plan that they had helped to devise.

The chairman closed the discussion by saying, "Since it is clear that the executive is divided, and that as outside directors we can't support this plan, I suggest you go back to the drawing board."

For four months, the three executive directors didn't talk about the débâcle. Consequently, the executive committee, comprising the three directors and four other senior executives, ceased to function properly. They only discussed trivia, avoiding any contentious issues.

The CEO's credibility was shot. The COO and the CFO went into "opposition" and produced an extremely watered-down investment plan, scarcely worthy of the name, but calculated to get board support.

Meanwhile, damaging rumours began to circulate in the organization. People saw memos alluding to the board meeting, and speculating on the motives of the CFO and COO in denouncing the original plan. Everyone knew that the investment plan, which had already been presented as a foregone conclusion, had been shelved – but nobody explained why. There were whispers that the CFO was in collusion with a competitor, who had already announced a major capacity expansion. Perhaps he was taking money from the competitor to stop further pipelines being laid. Some variants of the gossip had the COO taking money as well. Other hearsay was that the outside directors were on the take too.

The atmosphere inside head office turned nasty. The marketing manager developed severe migraines and was on sick leave half the time. The CEO started working very long hours, but also lunching with head hunters. He felt himself an innocent victim, but kept quiet about the board because he didn't want unpleasantness or the accusations getting out of hand. He suspected that the COO was after his job, and that the chairman might support a change.

Meanwhile, entering from stage left, came two leadership consultants. They had been contracted, before the fateful board meeting, to diagnose the leadership patterns of each of the executive committee members, and also to compile a group report. The consultants knew nothing about the board meeting and its dark aftermath.

The consultants' report revealed that one of the values espoused by the company and the executive committee was integrity – and yet that nearly all of the executive committee felt that integrity was conspicuous by its absence.

The executive committee members nodded sagely, but said nothing. Then the marketing man, the one experiencing the migraines, spoke up. The rules were that only the individual had access to their own reports, but could discuss their report with colleagues or the group if they wanted.

The marketing man began, "My report says that when there is conflict, my characteristic response, my 'racket' as they say, is to withdraw. I suppose my migraines have done that for me. I wonder if anyone else has anything to say."

"Mine is not too different," the CEO reported. "When things are going badly, I take it as my responsibility, and work harder on my own to sort things out. I guess things are not going to well at the moment. I can honestly tell you that I am worried sick and don't feel I can stick around much longer. Working harder on my own isn't producing the solution."

After this promising start, silence reigned again. Thirty seconds. One minute. Two minutes. It seemed like forever.

Finally, the PR manager, a tough lady, could stand it no more. "What is going on?" she demanded to the three directors. "Why haven't we been told what really happened at the board meeting? Everyone is asking me and they think I must know, and when I say I don't know, and haven't been told, they just don't believe me. They think there must be an awful secret hidden here. I can't bear for them to think that I'm lying to them, or that I'm part of a cover-up."

She had not done yet. Turning to the CFO, and fixing him with her steely blue eyes, she suddenly asked, "Are you a crook, Peter?" And swiveling round to the COO, "What about you, James?"

"No, I'm not a crook," Peter responded. "Me neither," James chimed in. And then everyone began to talk at once.

Six hours later the picture was clear to the whole meeting. The executive directors explained what had gone wrong. They had taken the board for granted, and not done their homework properly. Their reports of the competitor's planned new capacity were lower than the board believed. The executives' estimate of the market growth was higher. At the board meeting, the executives were not aware of the sources used by the outside directors. Having checked, they thought that the outside directors were probably closer to the truth – the merits of the investment were not so clear-cut.

No one had taken any money. The CFO and COO confessed to back tracking at the board, because new evidence came to light. The CEO accused them of treachery, but accepted their explanations. The CEO admitted that only his tendency to work out problems alone had stopped him asking for colleagues' help; it wasn't that he had any signs of corruption. The CFO and COO apologized to the CEO for not supporting him. The CEO apologized to everyone for keeping them in the dark.

The meeting, led by the PR manager and the marketing chief, agreed to accept the explanations, provided the CEO told the story in outline to the whole organization the following day. It had been a mutual failure of planning, not a conspiracy. The directors had since tried to work out things separately and not together. That was all now behind them. The CFO and COO supported the CEO, both in public and in private.

They didn't exactly all live happily ever after. But they got to grips with the issues, and started rebuilding trust. The modified, minor investment plan has been implemented. The same executives are still there, and the business is going well.

What is the leadership point of Rumpelstiltskin?

Naming the issue. Being able to say it. Having the courage to look the issue in the eye, to put it on the table. To talk about what everyone is aware of, to raise the obvious subject, concealed by mutual consent.

It should have been clear that Rumpelstilskin's code was his name. Once this dramatic glimpse of the obvious had been made, it was easy to discover the name, and make the horrid creature disappear for good. To name it was to solve it.

Yet how often do we all connive in keeping our dirty washing unwashed, locked away in a smelly closet? How dearly we love to avoid conflict, not to say something that everyone is thinking, but that will inevitably cause ructions?

In our experience, most leaders will do anything to avoid naming the issue, especially if it involves a close colleague. Chief executives will buy any amount of consulting, they will travel the world, they will do all manner of expensive and difficult things, they will engage in new initiatives, devise new strategies, institute change management programs, and even make major acquisitions. But they will not grapple with the issue that really matters. They will not name the issue. They will not ask if Peter is a crook, or if Neal ought not to retire, or if they should sell a major division. They will not name the issue confronting them. So it stays there, unnamed and unsolved, poisoning relationships, seeping ever deeper into the body of the firm, preventing its employees from realizing their potential.

KILLER QUESTIONS

What issue in your firm needs naming?

Yet naming the issue often makes it disappear. A short period of intense pain, followed by large amounts of peace and prosperity. Uttering the name of your Rumpelstiltskin is a great deal.

Smart things to say about leadership

"Most people avoid anxiety. Leaders name the issue behind it"

The executive who names the issue displays true leadership. That person may not be the official leader.

THE EMPEROR'S NEW CLOTHES

Based on the story by Hans Christian Andersen

A long time ago there was an emperor who was deeply vain and obsessed with his appearance. He spent all his money on new clothes, always seeking out the latest fashion from overseas.

So he was delighted when he was visited by two con men who claimed they were couturiers with the ultimate in high class apparel. They had the finest cloth imaginable, with fantastic colors and patterns but also – and this was the unique attribute – the magic power to appear invisible to anyone who was too stupid or not good enough for his job.

Psychologists and head hunters were clamoring for the cloth, the couturiers said, but seeing that the emperor was a man of great discrimination, they were willing to sell him the cloth, and to make it up for him exclusively. In fact, they said, the emperor or his senior officials could see the cloth being woven specifically to fit the emperor's dimensions.

So the emperor gave them a huge deposit, and they set to work on two looms. The emperor delegated his chief minister, a wise old man, to check on progress.

When he arrived at the weavers' workshop, he could see them working away, but he couldn't see the cloth. "Gosh," he thought to himself, "am I stupid and unfit to be chief minister?"

"Tell me, chief minister," demanded the con man who was weaving away, "what d'you think of it? Aren't the colors and pattern fantastic?"

The chief minister hesitated. Then he decided. He couldn't admit to being stupid and unfit for office. So he oohed and aahed over the cloth. "Magnificent. Cool. Wicked. What colors! What a fabulous pattern! I'll tell the emperor what a great job you're doing."

Other officials followed. They, too, couldn't see anything. But since the chief minister had seen the cloth, they assumed they had failed the test. None admitted it. Meanwhile, the story about the cloth and its magic properties had spread throughout the capital, and everyone looked forward to mocking anyone who couldn't see the clothes when they were worn.

When the emperor was brought the clothes, the weavers and all his officials lauded the finished articles to the skies. "Absolutely superb, your majesty." "Worthy of such a great monarch." "A real tribute to your discernment, sire."

Of course, the emperor couldn't see a thing, but he had to admit to himself that the clothes fitted snugly. He wore only his Calvin Kleins underneath the magnificent garments. "Light as a feather, they are," one of the couturiers exclaimed. At least the emperor could agree with that. He added, "What a fantastic fit!"

The page boys picked up the emperor's train, not daring to admit even to each other that they couldn't see a thing. What a godsend those mime classes were!

Everyone in the street cheered and praised the outfit. Nobody wanted to admit that they might be stupid or not up to their job. The emperor's fashion show had never drawn such enthusiastic crowds.

But stuck up a lamp post, a small boy from the countryside had gatecrashed the proceedings. He hadn't heard about the clothes' magic power to remain invisible. "Why's the emperor just wearing underpants?" he asked. "I know Calvin Kleins are trendy, but he hasn't really got the figure to show them off."

Slowly, the spectators around the little boy had to agree. "He's just wearing pants!" they shouted. "Pants! Pants! Pants!" More and more people shouted the refrain, as it rippled out into the main crowd.

Now the soldiers and police were getting restless. Should they turn the watercannon on the crowd? What if the emperor heard this treason?

But the emperor did hear. Sooner or later, everyone did. The emperor winced. The chief of police and the army commander approached the emperor, waiting for the signal to fire on the crowd. But he shook his head decisively. He went through with the procession, but vowed never to hold another, and not to buy more than one outfit a month. He even acquired an interest in social policy, and spent his money creating beautiful parks for all citizens.

When the small boy was brought before him, the emperor refused to banish or punish him. The boy later became famous for his TV inquisitions, when he was rude to all the richest and noblest of the land.

What do you make of that? What can leaders learn from this timeless story?

SMART REAL
LIFE STORIES
ABOUT
LEADERSHIP

BOO.COM

Boo.com was set up as Europe's leading Web-based supplier of fashion clothes. Boo was the brainchild of Swedish entrepreneurs Kasja Leander and Ernst Malmsteen and was backed by some of the smartest and most sophisticated investors around, including investment banks J P Morgan and Goldman Sachs, as well as Bernauldt Arnault, the LVMH fashion king, and the investment arm of Benetton.

The idea behind Boo was simple and convincing. The Internet was an opportunity to sell clothes to affluent younger people without the bother of shopping. It was quicker, cheaper, and more easily customized to each individual. Amazon.com had shown the potential in the less likely area of books. Now Boo would dominate the European market, and later the world market, creating a fresh brand and a new sense of excitement.

Because the key to future wealth was to be the biggest across the whole of Europe, Boo decided not to bother with testing the concept in one country. Instead, in the "land-grab" mentality then praised by the investment community,

Boo opened simultaneously in 18 countries, providing service in all their different languages. The software for this was developed by Boo at a cost of £35 million.

At first, everyone thought Boo a great idea. Even those who had their doubts hesitated to criticize Boo, for fear of looking old-fashioned.

On 18 May 2000, Boo announced that it was closing. Analysts, using hindsight, then reported that Boo's technology was too sophisticated for its target market of private households. They also drew attention to the lavish spending on first class air travel, top hotels, champagne receptions, and daily free fresh fruit and vegetables for Boo's 300-plus employees!

Boo defied many business conventions. It failed to test the concept before rolling it out. It failed to notice that successful Internet retailers of clothes in the US – and there are many – were also successful retailers with physical stores or else successful mail order houses. Like many dot-com start-ups, it failed to realize that making a profit, or at least being able to demonstrate that making a profit was possible at some time in the future, could be essential for further funding.

Boo was an honest enterprise, but it has much in common with the purveyors of the emperor's new clothes. Boo's backers believed an extraordinary story, that the old rules of business had been rewritten by the Internet. Were this story not believed by so many people, and supported by sky-high valuations of businesses that were clearly going to stay in losses for ages, nobody else would have believed it. The reasoning was circular, based on the blindness of consensus and the lack of vigorous dissent.

A small boy would have saved many sophisticated investors a packet.

Leadership, the emperor, and the small boy

The point is evident. The leader is the small boy, the person willing to take an unpopular view, honoring the still, small, voice of calm that the swirl and spin of business, especially in large organizations, can easily censor out. Leadership often does *not* require great intellect or sophistication, simply the refusal to go along with the herd, to state the obvious but unwelcome truth. Note also that leadership here does not need either status, or charisma, or any formal role, or any powers of persuasion. The small boy had none of these. What he had was authenticity and integrity, no less valuable for being the product of naïvety rather than of sophistication. Because what he said was so plainly true, despite being denied by everyone who had status and position, it could not be ignored. Once he made his statement, and it was clear that he would not shut up, the debate was over.

KILLER QUESTIONS

Where do you need a small boy? On what issue is there unanimous corporate groupthink that may be wrong?

Beware of the experts. The experts said the *SS Titanic* was unsinkable. On 15 April 1912 it sank – on its maiden voyage, with the loss of 1513 lives. When there is a corporate consensus that nobody questions, question it.

SMART REAL LIFE STORIES ABOUT LEADERSHIP

FINANCIAL SERVICES AND SUPERMARKETS IN NEW ZEALAND

A few years ago, one of us was working for the chairman of a successful and well-run supermarket chain. Everyone was very excited about the next big expansion plan, which was for the supermarket to offer a range of financial service products – loans and deposit accounts to start with, followed by insurance and home loans – to its customers. In the UK, Tesco and Sainsbury's, the two largest and most profitable chains, had made similar moves. An expensive and exhaustive consulting study had concluded that this was a huge opportunity. In fact, it was so good that the consultants had refused their large fee and wanted to be joint venture partners.

> I looked at the documents and concluded that the plan was flawed. I visited the chairman on a Sunday at his retreat by the sea and told him this. "I think I agree with you," he said. "But this thing has got so far, and everyone is so sure about it, that I don't think we can turn back now."
>
> It was a disaster. Eventually, a joint venture "partner" had to be paid to take the business away.
>
> Neither the chairman nor I listened to our own still, small voices. Such is the power of organizational groupthink. I like to think that if it happened again, one of us would insist on re-debating the issues, and aborting the project. But I am not sure.

What matters is not just the existence of the small boy, but that those in leadership positions heed what he says. The emperor could have quashed the dissent and executed the small boy. The leader's job is to search out the quiet voice of dissent. Everyone's job is to listen carefully to it.

The cult movie *Twelve Angry Men* is a perfect case where the still small voice is listened to – eventually. At first, it is clear that the accused youth is guilty of murder. Then, Henry Fonda tentatively puts another case. He finds one other member of the jury to support him – and then closed minds begin to open.

Yet often the small boy is not listened to. Such failures of leadership can have dire consequences.

Smart examples of missing leadership

> THE FIRST WORLD WAR
>
> Historians have long debated the origins of WWI. Certainly there were "profound" or "underlying" causes such as the tensions between the great powers of Europe. But such causes had existed for 20 years before war broke

out in 1914, without leading to general war. There were general causes of a similar nature in the Cold War during the 1950s and 1960s, yet there was not a nuclear holocaust.

What seems clear now is that decent and generally peace-loving men on both sides – particularly Sir Edward Grey, Foreign Secretary of Britain and Theobald von Bethmann Hollweg, the German chancellor, totally underestimated the consequences of war.

Previous wars had lasted weeks or months, not years, and although war was to be avoided, it would not be a catastrophe if it came. Sir Edward explained to the House of Commons on 3 August 1914 that, thanks to its Navy, Britain did not stand to suffer much more by entering the war than by standing aside. If "obligations of honour and interest" to Belgium were disregarded, British prestige would be damaged.[2]

David Lloyd George, the then British Chancellor of the Exchequer, later wrote to Mrs Asquith, wife of the Prime Minister, that Winston Churchill "dashed into the [Cabinet] room radiant, his face bright, his manner keen" at the prospect of war. "You could see he was a really happy man."

The liberal writer Thomas Mann, in Bavaria, was "grateful for the totally unexpected chance to experience such mighty events," and looked forward to Germany "smash[ing] the most despicable police state in the world," that is, Russia.

Though the preponderance of opinion everywhere was that war would have acceptable consequences, perhaps even welcome ones, there was at least one "small boy."

On 3 August 1914, Marcel Proust in Paris wrote to his agent, "Millions of men are going to be massacred in a War of the Worlds, like that of [H. G.] Wells."

On this occasion, nobody listened to the small boy. Even when it was clear, just months later, that Proust was right, still nobody in leadership positions listened. The consequences were the most horrific war in history, and, indirectly, the even more ghastly abominations visited on a hundred million victims by Lenin, Stalin, Hitler, and Mao.

All because decent leaders failed to listen. Like the emperor, they clothed themselves in a glorious illusion. Unlike the emperor, they then shut their ears to the still, small voice of reason.

THE WIZARD OF OZ

Based on the story by Lyman Frank Baum (1856–1919)

Once there was a small girl called Dorothy, who lived happily with her aunt, uncle, and her dog, Toto, on a farm in Kansas.

One day Dorothy and Toto were alone in the house when a whirlwind carried them away through the sky. Dorothy was frightened, but luckily they landed in a field full of flowers, to be greeted by the Good Witch.

"Where are we?" asked Dorothy.

"In the Land of Oz," the Good Witch replied. "Thank you for killing the Wicked Witch."

"What Wicked Witch?" enquired Dorothy.

"The one your farmhouse landed on."

So Dorothy looked under the farmhouse, and there she saw a dead Wicked Witch, and, a few inches from her feet, two magic shoes that had come off when the house hit the Wicked Witch.

SMART FAIRY
STORIES

Dorothy liked the shoes and put them on. They fitted perfectly. "They could come in handy some time," the Good Witch told Dorothy. "Remember that they can't be taken off the person who wears them, except if she agrees."

"Look," said Dorothy, "Toto and I would like to go home. How do we get there?"

The Good Witch was stumped. She had never heard of Kansas. She really didn't know what to say, but she had to say something. She thought of the most famous person she knew.

"You could try the Wizard of Oz," she told Dorothy. "Close by is the Yellow Brick Road, and that leads to the Wizard's head office. Yes, I'm sure the Wizard of Oz will help. He's a great leader, you know, everyone says so. He has his own City, the Emerald City, and the Emerald City Corporation is terribly successful."

Dorothy and Toto had no problem finding the Yellow Brick Road. Soon, they ran into a Scarecrow.

"We're off to the Emerald City, to see the wonderful Wizard of Oz," Dorothy told him.

"Jolly good," said the Scarecrow. "May I join you? My head is full of straw you see, and I'd like some brains, and I'm sure the Wizard will help."

So the Dorothy, Toto, and the Scarecrow marched happily together. Then they met a man made out of tin.

"I'd like to come too," said the Tin Man. "I want to ask the Wizard for a heart, so I can love."

A bit further down the road, they came across a big lion. It was more cuddly than scary, so they told him where they were going.

"Oh good," the lion said. "I want to come too, to ask the Wizard for some courage. Do you know, it's a real pain being a lion and not having courage."

So Dorothy rode on the lion, and the others all skipped along. They were getting on famously, and began to play nice games together. The Tin Man was getting fond of Dorothy, the Scarecrow had started reading the map, and the lion kept watch at night.

Eventually, Dorothy, Toto, the Scarecrow, the Tin Man, and the Lion all arrived together in the Emerald City. It was a pleasant enough place, all painted green, but when they were taken to see the Wizard, they were surprised and a bit disappointed.

From a distance, they heard a loud booming voice. "That the Wizard of Oz," they were told by the Emerald City guide who met them. "He's awfully famous and there's nothing he can't do."

But inside the Wizard's palace, all they saw was a tiny, wizened old man in a purple cloak. When he spoke, the Wizard had a soft, lisping voice, but it came out really loud and deep because he used a magic megaphone.

Well, Dorothy knew that you shouldn't judge by appearances, her aunt was always saying that. And the Wizard must be really important, because his public relations people kept rushing in and talking about the latest radio interview he had to do, or how the President of the United States wanted an audience with him.

The Wizard asked them each what they wanted him to do. "OK, I'll help you," he told them, "but first you must help me. I've heard that you, Dorothy, are good at killing Wicked Witches. Well, the local Wicked Witch is a real pest. So kill her and I'll help you all."

The Scarecrow, the Tin Man, and the Lion, as well as Toto of course, insisted on going with Dorothy to find the Wicked Witch. But when they saw her castle, they were all set upon by the Wicked Witch's flying monkeys, who flew them into the castle as prisoners. The Lion put up the best fight, but even he was carried off by the monkeys.

What do you think the Witched Witch wanted? Right, the bitch was after Dorothy's shoes. But Dorothy refused to give them, and because they were magic shoes the Wicked Witch couldn't prise the shoes off Dorothy.

Finally the Wicked Witch worked out how to make Dorothy co-operate. "Give me the ****ing shoes," she screamed, or I'll torture and kill Toto and all your ****ing friends."

Well, really, the Wicked Witch had gone too far. Dorothy was truly riled, and, without thinking, she seized a bucket of water and threw it over the Wicked Witch. And, strange to tell, the Wicked Witch began to disappear. "Aargh!" she said, "your water is killing me." And then she was gone.

While the lion kept the monkeys at bay, they all made their escape back to the Wizard of Oz, and told him their story. He was not a little surprised to see them back in one piece.

"Now it's your turn to help us please," said Dorothy. "You remember, a heart for the Tin Man, brains for the Scarecrow, courage for the Lion, and a first class ticket back to Kansas for me and Toto please."

Well, the truth is that the Wizard was a crafty old soul, but not all he was cracked up to be. He worked out that somehow the Tin Man already had grown a heart, and the Scarecrow had acquired brains, and the Lion seemed to him quite courageous. So he pretended to give them each what they asked for, and they were pleased.

But the Wizard had to admit that he couldn't run to airline tickets. He didn't even know what an airplane was, can you believe it? Finally he had to confess, "Look, I've helped all your friends, and I'd like to help you, Dorothy, but to be honest I can't."

"Oh shit," said Dorothy.

"Dorothy," the Scarecrow piped up, "how about using your magic shoes? Try asking your shoes to take you home."

"Now why didn't I think of that?" asked Dorothy and the Wizard both at the same time.

"Shoes, take me and Toto back to Kansas please," said Dorothy (she was usually polite and only used bad language under stress).

And suddenly she and the dog were back in their Kansas farmhouse with her aunt and uncle, who were amazed and ecstatic.

Dorothy and Toto lived happily ever after.

Pretty clear, huh?

AVOIDING THE JAPANESE ASSAULT

25 years ago, the flamboyant family founder of a photocopier firm retired. He had been very successful, taking the firm public and making it very valuable. But his firm was much smaller than the market leader and under attack from cheaper and more reliable Japanese machines in the segment of the market where the family firm specialized.

The founder decided not to pass on the firm's leadership to either of his two sons, and instead selected his daughter. The choice came as a surprise to everyone, because although she was bright and experienced, she was introverted. "She has negative charisma. She looks and acts like a librarian," one crony of the old man told him. "Yeah, but Sheila's the only one of my family that everyone trusts," he replied. "Besides, she still listens to me."

The leader timed his departure perfectly. In the next two years, the firm started to lose market share much more quickly to Canon, Ricoh, and other Japanese rivals. The board hired very expensive consultants to work out

SMART REAL LIFE STORIES ABOUT LEADERSHIP

what to do. The consultants were hired as a compromise, and to get an objective view, after furious rows between the two brothers. The consultants' study was going to take a year. In the meantime, the family firm's shares lost two thirds of their value and the financial community began agitating for a change.

After a particularly painful visit from her favorite financial analyst, Sheila, the CEO, decided to call her top team of three people together – herself, the CFO, Brian who was very bright but obnoxious, and John, the production director, who was popular with the factory workers but a bit dense, and whose business judgment was problematic. They were all siblings.

"Look," Sheila began, "our consultants are just two months into their study and say they need data about our relative cost position with the Japanese before they can recommend anything. They're off to Japan now. It'll be months before they'll say anything."

"I've just had a visit from an analyst who's made it clear that we will be taken over if we don't do something radical soon. The trouble is, brothers, I just don't know what we should do. I know normally we quarrel when we talk about strategy. John, I know you do it from the best of all motives, but you always protect the factory. Brian, you always provoke John, and I have to say, sometimes you provoke me too. I feel that you're much cleverer than me and I wish dad had given you my job. Can we please have a sensible and calm discussion without any games, because otherwise the family business is going to disappear."

Sheila's candor, for once, struck home.

Brian was first to respond. "OK, I'll try to be nice about it, but I can honestly tell you both this. We don't need to wait for the consultants. I don't know in detail about our costs versus the Japanese, but I can read a price list. They're 30% cheaper for a better machine. John, don't react, it's not your fault. Their models have 70% fewer parts than ours and their labor is cheaper. And because they share the large Japanese market, their volumes are much greater than ours, so their unit overhead costs are much lower. It's no surprise we can't compete. But I don't know what to do. If we close the factory, which is the right decision, and buy from the Japanese ourselves, the exit costs will be huge, and the unions will go on strike, so we'll lose the next few months' orders and most of our customers for good."

Instead of reacting instinctively to Brian's analysis, Sheila asked lots of questions and tried to see where Brian might be wrong. Meanwhile, John sulked. Four hours later, Sheila was satisfied.

When Brian went to the bathroom, Sheila said quietly, with as much authority as she could muster, "John, we have to face it: Brian's right. And if we turned ourselves into a sales and service operation, we could make higher profits than today. The figures prove it. We lose money making our machines but we make it on sales and service."

"OK" was all John said.

"This is where we need you," Sheila turned to John when Brian came back. "I think Brian is right. But can you get us out of manufacturing and avoid a strike?"

"Yes," said John. "If we're honest, and tell them the future of the family firm is at stake, I think I can do that."

"Great," said Sheila. "And Brian, if we do this, can you get the analysts off our backs, and avoid a takeover?"

"Probably," Brian replied.

And so peace broke out amidst the siblings. The plan worked. And when the consultants came back from Japan, they were surprised to find their bill paid and their work stopped. "I'm sure you've done the right thing," their vice president told Sheila.

Only the founder was furious. "How could you do this to me?" he angrily asked Sheila.

But three years later, when the shares were higher than ever, he told everyone it was his idea all along. "Got to move with the times, old boy," he told his crony. "Too many family firms get stuck in the past. Not us. Told you Sheila would shape up."

The answer lies within

Too often we think the answer lies outside our circle. We imagine that Tom Peters, or Jack Welch, or the Harvard Business School, or that very prestigious firm of consultants, or a book that has sold two million copies, or even our competitors have got the answer, and we haven't. *We* can't solve the problem. *They* can. Perhaps we can get their help.

Well, perhaps they can really solve our problem – at a price. Perhaps the right thing to do is to get outside help. But probably, if we really try, and are really honest, and make the best use of each other, the answer is within ourselves.

Too frequently, we become discouraged. We overlook what we have, what we've done, and who we are. Their grass is always greener; ours always looks parched. We should try watering our own grass. You get the hosepipe, I'll turn the tap, he can hold the hose. Maybe our grass can be greener than next door's after all.

KILLER QUESTIONS

What attribute do you lack? Who else in your team can supply it?

It's always easier to think the answer is external. It moves responsibility on to other shoulders. But this is the wrong place. Unless we take responsibility ourselves, we forfeit control of our destiny.

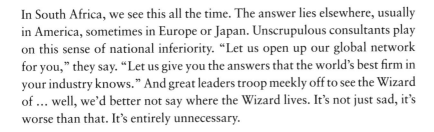

We must do it ourselves

"We cannot wait for great visions from great people, for they are in short supply. It is up to us to light our own small fires in the darkness."

Charles Handy

Smart quotes

In South Africa, we see this all the time. The answer lies elsewhere, usually in America, sometimes in Europe or Japan. Unscrupulous consultants play on this sense of national inferiority. "Let us open up our global network for you," they say. "Let us give you the answers that the world's best firm in your industry knows." And great leaders troop meekly off to see the Wizard of ... well, we'd better not say where the Wizard lives. It's not just sad, it's worse than that. It's entirely unnecessary.

I need you to be me

"Jung said that we need others to be truly ourselves. 'I' needs 'We' to be fully 'I.'"

Charles Handy

Smart quotes

The answer lies within – when we help each other, when we truly team up, body, brain and soul. It doesn't happen often. When it does, that truly is magic.

Notes

1 Taken from C. M. Woodhouse's introduction to the 1954 edition of George Orwell (1946) *Animal Farm*. The 1954 edition was a Signet Classic paperback, New American Library, New York. Mr Woodhouse originally wrote his article for *The Times Literary Supplement*, London, 6 August 1954.

2 This account, though not our interpretation of it, is taken from Norman Davies (1996) *Europe: A History*, Oxford University Press, Oxford, pp. 879–896.

6

The Practical Leader

"Nothing astonishes men so much as common-sense and plain dealing"

Ralph Waldo Emerson

So far Jon and Richard have had it all their own, and in my view, slightly academic way. My name is Robin Field and, while I do not share their academic credentials, I have had some experience of leading businesses. To a practitioner all this theory sounds a lot too easy. Life, day-to-day corporate as well as private life, just isn't like that. Among the slings and arrows of trying to keep the competition on the run, one's colleagues sharp and motivated and the shareholders supportive, it is not always easy to see the relevance of their highly-tuned advice on the psychological credentials of management theory.

All of what my collaborators say is very stimulating and a lot rings true to actual experience, but there are five major areas in which I think that the practice is a lot messier and more complex than their theory.

The first of these is the issue of leadership at all levels, to which some lip service was paid in the first chapter, but which then appears to have been lost in a welter of the doings of Henry Kissinger, Jack Welch and others with gold braid on their collars and thick carpet under their executive chairs.

The second is the question of management by consensus and some of the traps into which it has led me.

Thirdly, I'll deal with the importance of insight in leadership. Unless a leader knows something different from other people, or at least knows something with a rare degree of intensity, the best "leadership" skills will be sterile and ineffective.

My fourth theme is the impact of real life, of the arbitrary changes of exogenous events on all this theory. This will also lead us into consideration of how one should take decisions amongst all this uncertainty.

And finally, I want to explore the issue of self-awareness and what this means in practice: to what extent can a sufficiently stable map be drawn of ones own psyche to enable the sure plotting of the way forward that they recommend.

Smart quotes

Leaders and forked tongues

King Henry (in disguise): I myself heard the King say he would not be ransomed.

Williams: Ay, he said so, to make us fight cheerfully; but when our throats are cut he may be ransomed, and we ne'er the wiser.

Shakespeare, *Henry V*

I *Leadership at all levels*

The illusion of leading from the top

If we read any work on leadership, including most of the last six chapters, or look at the lives and achievements of the great leaders, we are in danger of falling into a fallacy. No organization of any size can be led just by the man or woman at the top. Leadership must take place at all levels and it is often most important and most difficult at the lowest.

A King or chief executive, isolated by reason of his seniority and by the trappings of power, can and frequently does get away with lousy human leadership in many respects. This is impossible for those in more approachable, vulnerable positions who must bear the day-to-day scrutiny of those reporting directly to them.

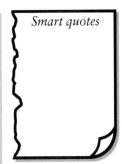

Smart quotes

The elusiveness of wisdom

"Who is wise?
He that learns from everyone.
Who is powerful?
He that governs his passions.
Who is rich?
He that is content.
Who is that?
Nobody."

Benjamin Franklin

The story of Arnold Weinstock – the invisible leader

Arnold Weinstock, the legendary managing director of the British electronics giant GEC (interestingly enough he always employed someone else to take the titular role of chairman), was said rarely to visit the component businesses in his empire. He had never met many of his senior managers and controlled his widespread and almost entirely provincial operations from his desk in central London through the minute and solitary perusal of financial reports.

Shareholders in what has now been more snappily renamed Marconi plc have reason to regret the more charismatic and fashionable form of leadership that succeeded him. Weinstock was not a very visible leader but he maintained a culture in which shop floor leadership, un-awed by a competing central figure, flourished.

The merchant navy – quiet leadership beats charisma

In the isolated and frequently highly-charged atmosphere of the merchant navy it has often been observed that those ships with the most detached, apparently uninvolved commanders have the strongest autonomous cultures and produce the most successful junior officers. The dashing, charismatic ship's master who is deeply involved in the social dynamics of his charges may look good personally, but frequently stifles the developing leadership abilities of those under his command.

I spent the beginning of my business career in ship management in the Far East where, time and again, we observed that those who clearly considered themselves to be – and often appeared to their contemporaries to be – the most active leaders, had the poorest record of inculcating leadership qualities in those serving under them. In contrast, those who appeared less satisfied with their own abilities often achieved most, both for their subordinates, and for the ship owners.

I remember in particular one very young master mariner, let's call him Peter, who was never very sure of his own abilities and used consequently to give his crew tremendous freedom of action within the rules. On one occasion Peter, with a bulk cargo of cement, brought his vessel alongside at a small port in the Philippines and in so doing, knocked over a brick wall, property of the port. Without a word of command, all Peter's off-duty crew were over the side and rebuilding the wall with their own cargo. By the time the port officials arrived, the wall was better than new.

Help! Leading a failing shipping agency

At the age of 26 I was promoted from ship management and sent to Taiwan to take charge of a shipping agency business. This business was clearly destined for the scrap heap, which was, I suspect, why muggins had been sent to sink with it. It had just lost its largest client, was under notice to lose its second largest, and was riven by systemic corruption.

I had not the faintest idea what to do. I couldn't speak the same language as the vast majority of my 200 colleagues, I had very little idea of what the business was meant to do, and had never managed even one business subordinate before. I was in no position to pretend to be an omniscient, charismatic leader.

I did, however, observe that whenever I succeeded, through the shadow of linguistic inadequacy, in asking a question, the senior staff of whom I asked it would always go and confer in their own tongue with the very junior women who worked the typewriters and telex machines. I wish I could say that I was smart enough to have fired those senior managers. The truth is that most of them, seeing the opportunity for bribes drying up, and the future prospects of the business growing less certain under this idiot neophyte foreigner, just drifted away.

I was then left with a business run almost entirely at clerical level. And guess what? Those female clerical staff, who knew how the business worked but had never before been given any autonomy, very quickly took on leadership roles and pulled the business up by its bootstraps. Within three years we had the largest and most profitable independent shipping agency in Taiwan. And we also had a lot of fun. I'm still in touch with some of the friends I made in those early, dicey days and they are all now very successful and fulfilled people.

Filofax – when the bosses knew worst

Again, when I blundered, more by good luck than judgment, into the chief executive's chair at Filofax in 1990 I saw a similar pattern. David Collischon had, in 1981, taken over a completely unknown company with no sales outside Britain and very few within. By 1987 he had built an internationally recognized brand with a sales presence in 50 countries around the world. He had then lost confidence in his own abilities and hired in a lot of high-powered "leaders" between 1987 and my arrival.

These people had all the right qualifications for leadership – they had taken the right exams and had no doubt read the right books. But they had forgotten that the most important leadership takes place not in the executive suite (and they had a very fancy one) but on the shop floor. Under them the company plunged from a net profit margin of over 20% into major losses.

Once again, the people who should really have been giving leadership, who actually knew how the business should work from day to day, were swamped with interference from on high, had their own autonomy taken away and were demoralized and emasculated.

It was not difficult to get things right. Remove the surplus layer of management – and with it some very surplus costs – allow the layers below to develop leadership roles and, with one or two strategic changes to product and positioning, hey presto! We had a winning business once again.

And if you are at the top, beware!

The great English statesman William Pitt said in 1770, "unlimited power is apt to corrupt the minds of those who possess it."[1] In 1887, in much snappier and more celebrated terms, Lord Acton wrote, "Power tends to corrupt and absolute power corrupts absolutely." Very few of the business leaders I've observed have been corrupt in the usual, financial sense. But nearly all of them have had considerable power, and power brings some unhealthy and insidious side effects – insulation from real life, people toadying to you, a tendency to believe your own propaganda, especially about your own merits, and a distorted view of reality, ranging from mild editing to complete derangement.

Jon and Richard tell us that leaders must be self-aware. True, yet paradoxically this is more difficult for powerful leaders than for lesser mortals. Those who have a lot to be humble about are better at humility than anyone who, for the time being, is reckoned to be a successful leader.

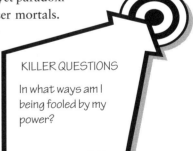

KILLER QUESTIONS

In what ways am I being fooled by my power?

But oh! How quickly things can flip-flop! To stay successful, I feel, you must disdain success, or at least your role in causing it. Others will exaggerate this; make sure you don't believe them.

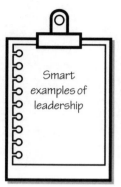

BOB NOYCE (1927–1990)

Robert N. Noyce is one of the greatest leaders of modern American business. Besides inventing the integrated circuit in 1958–9, leading Fairchild Semiconductor, and founding Intel in 1968, Noyce was an inspiration to a whole generation of creative Silicon Valley entrepreneurs.

I like Noyce because of his no-nonsense attitude towards leadership. He hired the best people and let them get on with it. Here's a story that reflects great leadership – and one that you can pinch for your own purposes:

"The young engineers who came to work for Fairchild could scarcely believe how much responsibility was suddenly thrust on them. Some 24-year-old just out of graduate school would find himself in charge of a major project with no one looking over his shoulder.

"A problem would come up, and he couldn't stand it, and he would go to Noyce and hyperventilate and ask him what to do.

"And Noyce would lower his head, turn on his 100-ampere eyes, listen, and say:

"'Look, here are your guidelines. You've got to consider A, you've got to consider B, and you've got to consider C.' Then he would turn on the Gary Cooper smile, 'But if you think I'm going to make your decision for you, you're mistaken. Hey … it's your ass.'"[2]

II *Don't be too consensual about consensus*

I am always very suspicious about management by consensus and feel convinced that for every story about success stemming from an internally generated harmony there are a dozen other untold tales of the same route leading to disaster.

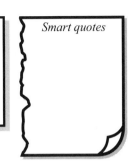

> ### Don't agree with me
>
> "Ah! Don't say that you agree with me. When people agree with me I always feel that I must be wrong"
>
> Oscar Wilde

Swedish consensus – good or bad?

Once Filofax had begun to be turned around we started to acquire a number of continental European subsidiaries, including one in Sweden. Our Swedish staff, of whom there were no more than a dozen, worked the shortest hours in the group. They arrived at 9.30 AM, had a long break for coffee and buns during at which they all sat down and chatted together from 11.00–11.45 AM, took lunch together from 1.00 to 2.30 PM, and all left the office at 4.30 PM.

A recipe for disaster?

Well, year after year this was the most profitable operation Filofax had by a long margin. Every decision was taken by consensus, everyone knew exactly what to do and why. Everyone believed in what they were doing and had the flexibility that comes from knowing precisely why they were doing it.

... and Danish consensus?

Soon after this we acquired a very similar subsidiary in Denmark. It worked in a similar way – though they worked much longer hours – but it consistently lost money.

Why?

The Danes also had a consensus. But it was the wrong consensus.

When we acquired them, they had their own brand of organizer. They all strongly believed in this brand, and promoted it alongside, and in competition with, the Filofax brand. When things went badly, their managing director was replaced twice, but the new managers were quickly converted to their colleagues' consensus.

The local brand was low-volume, and therefore expensive and unprofitable; it nevertheless occupied part of the market that should have been taken by our worldwide, high-volume, low-cost Filofax brand.

As I now realize, what I should have done, on day one, is take away their brand and say, "You can have any consensus you like, as long as it involves selling only the Filofax brand."

The story of the super-friendly firm

Even closer to home, some friends and I once started our own boutique investment business. We had all worked together in a similar firm where we had achieved great success. We chose from among our colleagues those whom we most enjoyed working with and who we thought could contribute most to the new venture. We had a relaxed, consensual working style in which we all, as a team, did exactly what work we enjoyed most.

I won't say it was a disaster, because it was a very pleasant way to pass a couple of years and we did, just, keep our heads above water. But the fire, the edge that is necessary to a first class business had gone out of us. We were all too busy agreeing with each other and dreaming up mutually supportive reasons for any failure for there to be any creative tension or forward dynamic. We moved from maximizing our opportunities to satisfying our comfort zones. And the curious sequel to this story is that since we decided that we could no longer afford this apparently enjoyable and self-indulgent lifestyle and gone our separate ways, all six of the principal partners in this business have individually and separately had marked success in different, more demanding activities.

Balancing consent and direction

How does one keep the balance between consent and direction? I guess that's a key part of leadership. Not being so close that you stifle initiative. Not being so detached as to abdicate responsibility.

Given that leadership is about change, it will almost always involve breaking an existing consensus in order to replace it with a new one. I have perhaps been very lucky in my management experiences in that time and again I have come into situations where autocratic and frequently wrong-headed management has stifled both initiative and consensus. Or perhaps it hasn't been such luck. Perhaps there is far more autocratic, hierarchical management practice in the world then we admit.

Europe and America – two different business worlds?

I have very little experience in the United States. Only twice have I been responsible for US businesses, both affiliates of European companies. Like many European managers I found these very testing experiences. Much has been written about the difficulties of American corporations in managing their European acquisitions and vice versa. In my limited experience one difficulty dominated all others.

Whenever I said to an American subordinate, "I think it might be a good idea to do the following," he or she agreed with me. It wasn't just that they did as I had suggested. They even dreamed up and told me a dozen reasons why I was right *even when they knew perfectly well that I was wrong.* The prevalent attitude appeared to be, "We are good soldiers, we will fall into line with whatever the boss says."

Here we have what is perhaps the most dangerous sort of consensus management: the false consensus in which everyone conspires to pretend to agree with the boss. Wherever you are, take pains to avoid encouraging this hypocrisy.

III   *Insight is inseparable from good leadership*

The best leaders I have observed *always* know and communicate some truth that is not generally appreciated. Leadership has a lot to do with pointing out the direction and getting people to follow, *but what really matters is that the direction is right.* You can appear to be a great leader, with huge charisma and communications skills, but if you are communicating the wrong message and leading in the wrong direction, then you are a failed leader. The road to failure in leadership can be paved with great charm and the best of intentions.

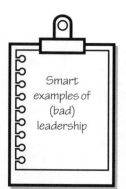

Smart examples of (bad) leadership

LORD LOUIS MOUNTBATTEN: TERRIFIC (BAD) LEADERSHIP

Louis Mountbatten looked like a great naval leader. He was tall and very handsome; he had lashings of charm and the ease of command that can only come from being born a Serene Highness and cousin of the King of England, and finding oneself husband of the greatest heiress of one's generation.

And he seemed to do all the right things: he would make it his business to know every man under his command personally and speak to each individually.

When the ship needed repainting no one was excused and his Lordship was over the side with his ratings with a paintbrush in his hand.

His men loved him and would follow him anywhere. And yet … he was a lousy captain. His first ship spent less than two months afloat in her year under his command. After a few days at sea, he killed one of his crew and nearly capsized the ship by pointlessly insisting on going far too fast in heavy seas.

Back to dry dock for six weeks. As soon as repairs were complete he steamed straight into a mine. Back again for three months. Then, on his way into the North Sea, he managed to collide with another ship. Back again for six weeks. Once again at sea he immediately contravened standing orders by sending humorous messages by Aldis lamp and so attracted the attention of an enemy U-boat. Back again to dry dock with a catastrophically damaged ship.

Mountbatten's leadership would have scored highly for technical merit, were it not a sequence of unnecessary disasters, all carried out, it is true, with the greatest gallantry, but also with the loss of other peoples' lives.

As Supreme Commander, South East Asia Command (SEAC), part of Mountbatten's mission was to assuage American concerns about British imperial ambitions. Yet he contrived to alienate, simultaneously, his American, Chinese, and Commonwealth allies, who contemptuously renamed SEAC "Save England's Asian Colonies."

The apotheosis of Mountbatten's career was the rushed and mismanaged partition of India, leading to the immediate massacre of over a million people, and an internecine struggle that still flares after more than a half-century.

This was a leader with a huge sense of duty, immense dedication, peerless mastery of the technicalities of his profession, and the ability to inspire ordinary men to follow him anywhere. But "anywhere" meant "to disaster." Lacking insight and the ability to make good decisions, he was a terrible leader.

The converse is also true: you can be very poor at human relations, lack charm and charisma, but if you have the right insight you can be a great leader.

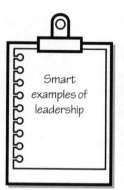

BILL GATES: LEADERSHIP BY BEING RIGHT

By all accounts Bill Gates was not the most popular boy in high school or the one voted most likely to succeed. Whatever polish he may have picked up later, when he dropped out of college to start writing software full time, he was not someone who would attract the devotion of his peers.

But Bill was right. He had a particular insight into the relative strengths of PC operating systems versus the hardware that they run on. It was an insight that had escaped the established leaders of the computer industry. And guess what? The awkward, nerdy, college drop out from Seattle is today acknowledged throughout the world as the single greatest business leader of his generation.

ANDREW CARNEGIE (1835–1919)

Born in Dunfermline, Scotland, the son of a desperately poor weaver who emigrated to Allegheny, near Pittsburgh, in 1848, Andrew Carnegie was the model "smart young man" who went from rags to fantastic riches. Hired as a teenage telegraph messenger, he mastered telegraphy and from the age of 17 made himself indispensable to Tom Scott, a railroad magnate. Andrew Carnegie triumphed as a manager and an investor.

In his thirties, he was already quite rich – but unfulfilled. Around 1870, he became obsessed with steel. Before he entered the steel business, he realized two things. One, that steel would change the physical basis of the world. And two, that the secret of making money in steel was to have higher production volumes than anyone else.

"Cheapness," Carnegie said, "is in proportion to the scale of production … the larger the scale of operation the cheaper the product."

His formula for success: "Cut the prices; scoop the market; run the mills full… Watch the costs and the profits will take care of themselves."

Carnegie communicated his insight relentlessly, telling his managers, "Run our works full; we *must* run them at any price … keep this in mind – all other considerations secondary."

Carnegie's insight was new and fresh – and he acted upon it consistently for thirty years, becoming one of the planet's richest people as a result. He spent money to save money. He hired the best engineers to build the lowest-cost mills. He kept telling his people that only the slimmest margins were necessary. Keep margins and prices low. Grow the market. Benefit from even greater scale economies. Have larger plants and lower costs than any competitor.

To build his first mill, he used all his available cash and borrowed heavily. He outspent all rivals on capital expenditure, in depressions as well as in good times. He inspired all his people with one simple idea – get and keep the lowest costs for producing steel.

He was a great leader, because he was right.

I like the story of Andrew Carnegie because his style of leadership was so purely based on knowing, and acting on, a couple of great truths. Carnegie was an able and flamboyant man, but what mattered was that he led in the right direction. He was an enthusiast and a visionary – one whose vision was right – and that was enough. He did not work very hard. As soon as he had any money, he traveled the world and always took long vacations.

Written reports were all that kept Carnegie in touch with his burgeoning business empire when he was away for months at a time. Imagine it. No phones, no faxes, no email, no video links. Invisible leadership at its most

What do you know that other people don't properly appreciate? What is the insight at the core of your leadership?

wonderful. Carnegie knew he had a formula for success, and he communicated it effectively. He proves that you can be economical with leadership and still be a great leader.

IV *Events and how to harness them*

"I claim not to have controlled events, but confess plainly that events have controlled me"

Abraham Lincoln

Insight is invaluable; but so too, in a way, is its opposite. Every effective leader I can recall was also opportunistic. Objectives were clear; but the means to realize them were infinitely flexible.

Dick in Hong Kong – the Houdini of relationships

As a young man I briefly shared an apartment in Hong Kong with a very ambitious and subsequently highly successful American whom I shall call Dick. We were both bachelors and Dick, like many of the colony's affluent young executives, was very sought after by the ladies. As a consequence he was continually getting himself into what appeared to be completely untenable positions; Dick would be committed to taking two girls to dinner on the same night, or he would agree that a longstanding girlfriend from the

US should come to stay when a local girl of more recent acquaintance was already living with him.

It may well be that in less sheltered circumstances than those in which I have lived, young men are always getting themselves into such scrapes, but the remarkable thing about Dick was that he never worried about them and never appeared to do anything in advance to ward off the impending catastrophe. And yet, somehow, it never happened. Events would always fall out, often at the last minute, so as to avoid the danger; one of the potentially clashing dinner guests would fall sick, or the visiting girlfriend's airplane would be delayed by an unforeseen pilots' strike until just after the local companion had left on holiday.

It wasn't the case that Dick led a charmed life and that he just sat back and let all this happen. He may not have *appeared* to do anything to avoid catastrophe but he ruthlessly exploited those opportunities that fate offered him, to mould the future to his will. With a deceptively casual touch here and a word there he would selflessly agree that if young Mary felt a chill coming on she really should stay at home. He let Susan know just in time that in view of the impending strike, she (much as it would pain him) should consider postponing her departure. He didn't know what gifts the gods would throw him but when a gift arrived he had so clear a vision of how his life should be that he could use it without delay or confusion.

So Dick would sail imperturbably through. I have no doubt that Dick is carrying on his apparently charmed and imperturbable existence at the top of the major international company he now runs.

Now, I am not recommending that one should leave one's business life to chance or that one should deliberately set up impending disasters in order adroitly to side step them at the last minute. But it may be true that there is a little too much planning in business, a little too often the assumption that every possible future scenario can be modeled, so that when things turn out differently, as inevitably they will, the leader is left floundering.

Be ready for the unexpected, not in terms of having planned every possible permutation of events but by being sufficiently detached from the planning to be able to react. As an earlier chapter put it, leadership is about seeing things as they are, not as how you want them to be. But it is also, overwhelmingly, about retaining a clear vision of how, given all the new data, things should be and moving one's world towards that.

The opportunity presented by imminent disaster

It is often only when things go wrong that the most powerful leadership potential can emerge. Without Hitler and World War II, Winston Churchill would be remembered, if at all, as an obscure and self-important politician, scion of a formerly great military and political dynasty, who failed to retain office through his unfortunate predilection for falling out with his closest allies.

Disaster leads to leadership

"At last I had authority to give directions over the whole scene. I felt as if I were walking with destiny, and that all of my past life had been but a preparation for this hour and for this trial."

Winston Churchill, on being made Prime Minister on Britain's darkest day, June 10, 1940.

Fortunately, in business things are always going wrong, or at least have the potential to do so. The commercial world moves faster and faster. As the world grows smaller, more and more random events can impinge on any business decision. The leader has more noise to cope with, consequently more potential triggers for change and therefore for success.

Life is difficult

"Life is difficult. This is a great truth, because once we see this truth we transcend it. Once we know that life is difficult – once we truly understand and accept it – then life is no longer difficult. Because once that is accepted, the fact that life is difficult no longer matters."

M. Scott Peck

How does one remain sufficiently detached from the day-to-day turmoil, from the management role of keeping the ship upright to interpret all this data and plot a course for the future?

When a problem arises and the answer doesn't …

In my last year or so at Filofax I was able to delegate all the company maintenance tasks and spent a great deal of time trying to detach myself from day-to-day distractions by reading books and magazines and meeting people from outside our industry. We had a huge strategic issue: although our industry looked healthy and we dominated it in terms of brand recognition and market presence, I knew, from the moment that the Palm Pilot was launched in 1996, that conventional paper-based organizers were doomed. For more than two years I struggled with this issue. But it wasn't until after, with a stroke of providential timing worthy of my old friend Dick, we had been able to sell the business at the end of 1998, that suddenly and unprompted the answer came to me. It had been under my nose for years. And the beauty of it was that it was most attainable when we needed it most.

Filofax had the best name in the world in paper-based agendas. Just as these were about to fall from supremacy, the World Wide Web had emerged with incredible speed and with unprecedented investor enthusiasm. Web-based agenda systems desperately needed a marketing platform to reach consumers throughout the world. They had almost limitless amounts of cash to invest. I don't say that an alliance with Filofax would have necessarily been of vast long-term benefit to the unfortunate shareholders in these Internet start-ups. But it would certainly have been a shot in the arm for Filofax.

But try as I did to detach myself, I was so close to the problem that I couldn't see the solution. All the noise from the technology sector seemed to be antipathetic to us. Yet in these external and apparently harmful events was a key to our future.

I don't say it was *the* key because, as St John's Gospel reminds us, "In my father's house are many mansions." There is not only one route to success and life won't stand still while we try them all. Leadership is about choosing one, and inspiring everyone else to come down the same route.

Making decisions under uncertainty

My collaborators have certainly pulled no punches on just how difficult many decisions are. They have even offered a whole host of methodologies to assist the puzzled leader. Exploration, Pass to the Right, Deep Democracy, the dishing out of De Bono's six hats – all have their value, but they can also share a nasty downside. In revealing to your subordinates that you, too, are uncertain of the right path, you risk frightening them and casting doubt on whatever route is eventually chosen.

In F. Scott Fitzgerald's last, unfinished novel, *The Last Tycoon*, the central character, a business leader, tries to explain to the pilot of his airplane the secret of his success. He points to the mountains over which they are flying and says:

"Suppose you were a railroad man. You have to send a train through there somewhere, and you find there are three or four or half a dozen gaps, and not one is better than the other. You've got to decide – on what basis? You can't test the best way – except by doing it. So you just do it." The pilot thinks he has missed something, that there is some trick he has not understood. But the tycoon simply says, "You choose one way for no reason at all – because that mountain's pink or the blueprint is a better blue."

There is often no rational way for the leader to choose. Yet choices have to be made and the leader has to make them and to carry all his colleagues with him. If he exposes to them his own uncertainty or the arbitrariness of his choice he will lose them. He has to make the choice and carry the consequences, not being afraid, if the choice turns out to be wrong, to say, "Sorry guys, I got it wrong, but *now* I know the right way."

And there are many more decisions of this sort than management books would have us believe. If every time we involve others in these uncertainties we risk distracting them from a clear vision of what they have to achieve. The buck has to stop somewhere and it stops with the leader. In many cases there is never going to be a rational basis for decision but often *any* decision, any instruction to the people at the sharp end, is better than no decision.

Leaders cultivate luck

Luck plays a greater role in many careers than it is fashionable to admit. Luck upsets all our Protestant, rational training in hard work, merit and reward.

Yet what is luck but a propensity continually to take in all the data, free oneself from prejudice and try again? It is a propensity to positive action, to change, to grasping the initiative.

The only certainty we have in business today is lack of certainty; the only immutable is constant change. In this environment a willingness to take de-

Smart quotes

<u>Don't care about success</u>

"Don't aim at success – the more you make it a target, the more you are going to miss it. For success, like happiness, cannot be pursued; it must ensue, and it only does as the unintended side effect to a cause greater than oneself or as the by-product of surrender to another person.

"Happiness must happen, and the same holds for success: you have to let it happen by not caring about it. I want you to listen to what your conscience commands you to do and go on to carry it out to the best of your knowledge. Then you will live to see that in the long run – in the long run, I say! – success will follow you precisely because you had forgotten to think about it."

Viktor E. Frankl[3]

cisions, to promote change is going to win more often than it loses. On more occasions than I can enumerate I have taken decisions, great and small, on what seemed to be the best data available and have found that the data was wrong but the decision right.

At Filofax we shifted some production from China to India because we believed that the US dollar, in which we bought leather goods from China, would strengthen and that we could find the same grade of leather in India. In fact the US dollar weakened and the leather we had been promised was not available in production quantities. But the alternative Indian leather we were offered was so unusual and distinctive that it spawned a whole new, and highly successful, family of products.

Of course, not all these 50/50 decisions will work out, but a culture in which the leader is ready to admit mistakes and to move on, a culture that is prone to action rather than caution, is more likely to win today and tomorrow.

Why can't leaders be honest?

One of the many difficulties I had when running a public company was that whenever – as inevitably happens from time to time – we had taken a wrong route, I wanted to say not only to my colleagues but to my stockholders in the annual report, "I got that one wrong and we are now going to do it differently."

Every time the non-executive directors and stockbrokers would rein me back: "You mustn't frighten the market by admitting to be fallible." If business leaders would admit to a little more fallibility perhaps investors, who are fallible too, would be more inclined to trust them.

V <u>*The impermanence of the self*</u>

But which self should you be true to?

Jon and Richard, as well as Polonius in the extract on the left, have given excellent advice about being one's self and acting from the firm foundation of self-awareness. But who is that self and how firm is that foundation?

There are some issues, like integrity, that are indispensable and immutable. But many other aspects of our characters and our awareness of them are continually changing. At least that's true in my own case. Here I am, almost 50 and I am forever being surprised by aspects of my own character that I didn't know I had.

My collaborators appear to see this process in a rather negative light, for example identifying one's "racket" so that one can avoid the traps into which it might lead one. But I have found that learning more about my own psyche has been positive and has enabled me to open new doors and exploit potential that I didn't know I had.

For example, when I was about half way through my business career a new colleague, who subsequently turned into a very close friend, said to me, "You're a bit of a performer aren't you? You should use that more." Now I had always considered myself a rather shy and awkward person, had avoided any public appearances and had constantly pushed subordinates forward to make announcements, rally the troops or present the prizes.

As a result of this unsolicited throwaway line, I began to take the stage a little more, and guess what? I enjoyed it, those I worked with appeared to appreciate it, and I discovered a whole new dimension to my own personality and to leadership.

How can you learn more about yourself? You guessed it: by listening. As we said earlier, a key part of the skill-set that is leadership is communication and at least half of successful communication is active listening; listen to learn more about your business, listen to learn more about your subordinates and, above all, listen to learn more about yourself.

But what will you hear? Unless you actively encourage those around you to give straight feedback you will hear nothing but polite platitudes. As we point out elsewhere, one of the dangers of a leadership position is that so many people appear to have a vested interest in lading you with flattery that there is a very real danger that you will start to believe a self-serving myth. A critical spouse and children to bring you down to ground are helpful here.

Not all of us are lucky enough to have this self-adjusting mechanism and there is at least one other trick that can help. First, ensure that as part of the performance review process of your colleagues who report directly to you, there is also an upward review of your own performance. I find that this formal, two-way process is helpful throughout a firm. Some subordinates will flatter, but in my experience the best can be brutally honest.

Second, however exalted ones leadership position, until one reaches that of God, one will always come into contact with peers, or at least contacts outside one's own organization. Ask their views. I used to ask for feedback from our stockbrokers, from institutional investors and from non-executive directors. A lot of this was useful and occasionally some was alarming. Even when no more than platitudes come back the process of asking is always helpful in cementing a relationship.

Leadership is about learning and changing, and the more you learn about yourself, and the more you change, the more effective you'll become. By all means, learn about your "rackets," but more importantly, learn about the one or two things that you're really great at. Do more of these things, and do them even better than before, and you really will be away to the races.

Notes

1   Speech by William Pitt to the House of Lords, 9 January 1770.

2   Tom Wolfe (1983) The Tinkerings of Robert Noyce, *Esquire,* December, 1983.

3   Viktor E. Frankl, Preface to 1984 edition of *Man's Search for Meaning,* Touchstone, New York.

7

Finale – The Paradoxes of Leadership

"None will improve your lot
If you yourself do not"

Bertolt Brecht

Leadership is not what is seems. The truth about leadership is full of paradox. In sum, let's revisit and elaborate six essential points that are less simple than they first appear.

I The purpose of leadership is progress

This is the nobility of leadership: making the world a better, richer place. Leadership is creative. In business this means creating wealth – through doing things differently and better, through finding different things to do, and through doing things with fewer or cheaper resources. And business leadership is perhaps the most important form of leadership, because it eliminates poverty and creates the material underpinning of civilization.

Leadership is "contrary." It does not maintain the status quo. It does not allow people to carry on as they always have. It sees potential – and makes people realize that potential, often against their natural inclinations. Leaders take people somewhere they haven't been, and would never go on their own.

II The two sides of leadership: insight and self-awareness

Effective leaders have two essential attributes – insight and self-awareness. The two are quite different. One without the other is useless.

Insight is knowing something useful that other people don't.

I can have terrific charisma, charm, powers of persuasion, maturity, self-awareness, humility, wonderful technical skills, and be the world's best manager – yet if I have no insight, I am not a leader. Without insight, there's no beef in the leadership bun.

In business, insight means knowing how to create wealth. Knowing a way that is different or better than anyone else's way. And being able to describe this to other people – either through a hard-edged blueprint, or through a more blurred, yet powerful, vision – so that they can create wealth.

Anyone without insight, or the ability to generate insight, should not aspire to leadership. Stick to something easier, such as management or being an expert.

Self-awareness is knowing who you are and having the integrity and personal qualities necessary to lead. To explain more concretely ...

III   *Self-awareness: the elusive soul of leadership*

Effective leaders have a bundle of personal attributes that can best be encapsulated as "self-awareness."

Smart quotes

Self-awareness includes honesty and integrity; being willing to engage and take responsibility; facing unpleasant facts and confront anxiety; being able to subordinate a powerful ego; tolerance of ambiguity, tensions and contradictions; versatility and the ability to deploy a wide variety of attributes, each at the right time; skill at listening and learning; knowing when to act and when to hold back; being accepted by the group and able to persuade it; being able to develop oneself and other people; and confidence in one's individuality.

AYN RAND (1905–1982)

The individualistic writer and philosopher, Ayn Rand, makes one very useful point about leadership and life. Her message is that leaders must be *individuals* and not conform to society's template for leaders.

In her 1938 fable *Anthem*,[1] describing a backward totalitarian state of the future, the Council of Vocations:

"came to give us our life Mandates which tell those who reach their fifteenth year what their work is to be for the rest of their days …

"And the Council of Vocations sat on a high dais, and they had but two words to speak to each of the Students. They called the Students' names, and when the Students stepped before them, one after another, the Council said: 'Carpenter' or 'Doctor' or 'Cook' or 'Leader.' Then each Student raised their right arm and said: 'The will of our brothers be done.'

"… if the Council has said: 'Leader,' then those Students go into the Home of the Leaders, which is the greatest house in the City, for it has three stories. And there they study for many years …"

The Council of Vocations and the House of Leaders were intended to turn out homogeneous leaders devoid of any spark of individuality. Ayn Rand's tale attacked communism and Nazism, when leadership was institutionalized and unthinking obedience to the state was required. What possible relevance has this to our own days?

We are struck by how stylized our conceptions of leadership are, and by how homogeneous most leaders of large corporations appear. We know a large number of individual business leaders, and how diverse they really are. Yet when they get to the office, when they chair meetings, when they talk to financiers, when they report to the stock market, when they address public meetings, when they communicate to their employees, these individuals are all too often interchangeable, gray, and predictable. The Canned Role dominates the individual identity – a sure sign that leadership will be conspicuous by its absence.

Top leaders live within a system that limits their idiosyncrasies. They are trained in the same few top universities and business schools. Their firms are audited by the same few top accounting firms. They are advised by lawyers and corporate financiers and communications experts all working to the same rules and regulations. They lunch with the same kind of people as themselves. They are cut off from the real world by secretaries, assistants, large cars and sometimes even their own airplanes. If they start as colorful individuals, they still end up as gray replicas of each other. And they are nearly all middle-class, middle-aged men.

Our market system encourages individuality in entrepreneurs, but not in successful corporate leaders. Once a corporation becomes large and successful, individuality goes out the window. This is one reason why corporations wax and wane. Individuality is essential for creating new success. Corporations and stock exchanges create systems that constrain individuality at the top.

The more successful they become, the greater the pressure on leaders to conform, to tone down their personality, to become part of a machine. Yet the more leaders conform, the more they live off the past rather than create the future.

Henry James criticized the painter John Singer Sargent for having "a certain excess of chic and not enough naïvety." Many top executives exude sophistication and urbanity, yet they might as well have come straight from Central Casting. Are you a representative of the elite, or totally your own person?

> The essence of leadership is individuality. To protect and renew your individuality, refuse to listen to the conformist advisers, find unusual and different people to talk to, and constantly search for new truths and new directions. These are unlikely to emerge while you are working in the office.

Self-awareness does not mean that you must be a saint – in business, this is not a formula for success – but it does mean you need to have unusual personal qualities. It means being "semi-detached" – able to step out of yourself and out of any particular time and place. It means having degrees of complexity, self-knowledge, and emotional intelligence that are well above average, *and* being true to yourself and everybody else.

In these pages we've seen some surprising paradoxes of self-awareness – and they're worth highlighting again:

- *Leadership requires intelligence, yet extraordinary intelligence is rarely combined with self-awareness.*

  Why not? Because self-awareness is fed by new data, by listening, by being willing to be embarrassed. High intelligence is a shield against such indignities. Those who know a great deal usually feel a below-average need to learn. The smarter you are, the more you need to work on your self-awareness.

- *A strong ego is necessary to give the confidence to lead, yet a strong ego stops you appreciating what's really going on.*

  When you're really good, it's hard to be humble too.

  One of the worst problems that successful business leaders have to face (and usually fail to face) is their power, their reputation, and their advisers. Power may not corrupt, but it isolates and fools. Business culture does not encourage frank admission of mistakes, yet without honesty and openness it is difficult to understand what is happening.

- *Self-awareness means both accepting yourself and not being satisfied with yourself.*

At some deep level, the leader must believe that he or she is "OK." Yet the leader must also be aware of his or her "rackets," the destructive and habitual instinctive patterns of behavior that we all have, that afford us short-term relief at the expense of deepening and prolonging the underlying problem. The leader must be adept at delving within himself or herself, fully and fearlessly confronting what is dysfunctional because, whatever bad things are found, they do not compromise self-acceptance.

The leader must therefore be optimistic about "re-deciding" what has been decided in early childhood, while not denying the need to do so. The leader must be restless and self-demanding, yet also at peace.

Self-development for leaders is not expensive self-indulgence. It is a small price to pay for having an effective leader.

- *Self-awareness demands the willingness to confront the anxieties that others would rather sweep under the carpet, yet this is usually the last thing people want from their leaders.*

People want a sense of security; yet real security requires a deep acknowledgement of what is going wrong, so that it can be neutralized or transcended. Security requires anxiety. Therefore, leaders must be willing to be unpopular. They must often be the bearers of bad tidings – naming the issue that everyone is studiously ignoring, or saying that the emperor has no clothes, when the emperor may not be a person, but rather the organization itself. Yet, because they are trusted, leaders are the acceptable face of the unacceptable.

- *Another paradox of self-awareness is that leaders must be guileless and yet artful.*

Integrity is absolutely essential for trust, yet the leader cannot reveal the truth, the whole truth, and nothing but the truth. This is not just for reasons of state, or to protect individuals' privacy. It may also be because the leader has no confidence that the course she is setting is right. In the absence of knowing precisely what to do, the leader must absorb anxiety – paralysis is not conducive to survival.

- *The final paradox is inherent in our "triangle of tensions."*

The leader has to cope with the contradictions between who he or she is, the Canned Role or obligations that the organization imposes, and the emergent process of markets, competition and events.

These tensions can tear a person apart. The clear implication – but one that is rarely drawn – is not only that leadership is difficult, but also that it may be an impossible task unless the individual is unusually fitted both to the organization and to the task ahead.

If the disparity is too great between who the leader really is, and what the company expects, then the leader cannot be himself or herself at work. This inevitably leads to a failure to practice what you preach. And that leads to corrosive cynicism and lack of confidence in the leader.

Even if the leader and the organization are well suited to each other, the leader must also be well fitted to the emergent process – to what is about to happen in the messy reality swirling around the firm. This goes back to the point about insight being essential. If the leader has the wrong insight, or none at all, then two sides of the triangle of tensions will become increasingly detached – sinking the leader.

The conclusion we draw is this – think three times about becoming, or remaining, a leader. The right leader is wonderful, but rare. The wrong leader is a recipe for unhappiness, both for the leader and for the whole organization.

CHARLES HANDY

Charles Handy (born 1932) represents the "civilized tendency" of business thinkers. Son of an Irish Protestant minister, with previous careers as a Shell International expatriate in Malaysia, an economist, and at London Business School and MIT, Handy is now the writer and broadcaster who always asks "Why?"

Handy has three things to tell us about leadership. One is his emphasis on the "representative" role of the leader, and the way that this conflicts with the role of chief executive:

"Leaders, to be effective, have to represent the whole to the parts to the world outside. They may live in the centre but they must not be the centre. To reinforce the common cause they must be a constant teacher, ever travelling, ever talking, ever listening, the chief missionary of the common cause. This role sits ill with that of chief executive …"[2]

A key part of the leader's role, he insists, is to run "popular teach-ins," to "carry the people with them."

Second, Handy stresses the leader's role in developing and promoting the "common cause," the purpose of the organization: "[the common cause] can

SMART PEOPLE
TO HAVE ON
YOUR SIDE

look like waffle, and sometimes is. Properly done, it is not waffle but the glue of the enterprise."

Third, we should reach back to Charles Handy's second book, *Gods of Management*, published in 1978.[3] Here, Handy delineates four types of organization, and, by implication, leader:

- The *Zeus* cult, where the leader sits at the center of a web and controls things. The Zeus enterprise is a club centered on the leader; influence is measured by how near executives are to the leader and how much time the leader spends with them. Zeus often characterizes young, entrepreneurial firms, professional service firms, family firms, and those in sport and performing arts.
- The *Apollo* cult, where role is everything. This is the classic bureaucracy found in large organizations and especially in the public sector, monopolies, and insurance companies.
- The *Athena* culture, which is based on specific professional expertise (Athena was the patron saint of craftsmen and explorers), problem solving, and team-work, and is most often found in "knowledge industries" such as software or consulting
- The *Dionysus* culture: existential, super-individualistic, anarchic, where the leader's role is "herding cats." Found in universities, research firms, and small firms organized around one or more creative individuals.

As Handy says, any organization can be recognized as falling primarily into one of these categories.

So what? Well, one clear implication is that a leader must recognize his or her fit and empathy with each style – or lack thereof. New leaders parachuted into a different kind of organization must recognize the differences. If they are strongly marked, the leader is unlikely to be effective. Only in an emergency, and by bringing in new senior people with the leader's own bias, or else by operating stealthily over a long time period, can the leader hope to change the culture. Even then, acceptance by existing executives will be problematic.

Another thing that follows from the "gods" is that the leader must be aware of what style he or she *wants* for the organization, and the extent to which this is different from current reality. The style that is appropriate may legitimately be influenced, to a degree, by the leader's own proclivities, but a key question is, "what type of cult is most likely to lead to success for the firm?"

Nowadays it is fashionable to have a tolerant, "it all depends" attitude to such questions. Academics call it "contingency theory" – firms evolve particular styles according to their history and the environment. This has some truth, yet can be a cop-out. Some styles are much more successful than others, at the same time, in the same market, in the same place.

For example, the three authors of this book have worked in consulting firms that each worshipped one of Handy's four different gods. We have no doubt that Athena is the best style for consulting, followed by Zeus (effective but very difficult to manage the transition from the first leader), then by Dionysus, and lastly by Apollo.

This is not a universal ranking of desirability, and leaders don't need one. They should just observe which of their direct and relevant competitors are most successful, the styles that they have, and whether their own firm could evolve that way.

Moving a firm from one style to another is a tricky and slow process but it may be one of the leader's most important and enduring tasks. This is probably Jack Welch's most important legacy – getting GE to follow Athena instead of Apollo.

On the other hand, for every leader we know who has successfully transformed a culture, we know at least three or four who have tried and failed. Leading a culture that is out of synch with both your style, and that required for success, is usually a thankless and futile task. The chances are that your talents would be more constructively used elsewhere, so think hard before taking a job with an organization whose cult is different from yours.

IV Leaders develop strong personal relationships

At the heart of leadership power is the ability to develop and nurture trusting relationships with other high quality individuals, both inside and outside the organization.

Smart quotes

> ### Individuality requires relationships
>
> "Paradoxically, it is the relationship that allows individuality to emerge, that spawns the self-acceptance necessary for discovery of – or, better, recovering or uncovering – one's creative potential.
>
> "Only by being willing to be oneself in a relationship, by accepting one's own difference and having it accepted by another, can one discover the creativity and strength to change."
>
> Robert Kramer[4]

The most effective way for you to realize your innate leadership potential is through one-to-one relationships where there is two-way learning and deepening mutual respect and trust. Just as public speakers addressing a large audience are trained to talk, at each moment, to one person in the audience, so too the only way for leaders to influence many people is to realize that they must do so through influencing *individuals*, who themselves will then influence other people.

A leader's one-to-one relationships take many forms – ranging from "master–apprentice" training and mentorship to peer-group collegiality, where the leader is genuinely "first among equals." Yet *all* successful relationships are based on the same fundamental principles of *yin* and *yang*, underpinned

> Relationships change identity
>
> "Recognising who a person wants to be ... is the key ... What
> motivates people varies according to what they want, and what
> they want varies according to what they want to be ... A leader
> ... must take into account the identity being sought by a person,
> what this identity already is and where it is going – identity is
> work-in-progress."

by mutual care and respect, trust, and reciprocity, augmented by humor,
fun, and play.

For the "Learner Leadership" model – discussed in Chapter 4 – to work,
individuals must be committed to each other's development as people and
therefore as leaders. The ability to build relationships and develop potential – of oneself, of other individuals, of teams, of organizations, and of
the economy and society – is more than a skill. It requires integrity, yet it
requires more than integrity. It requires *competence* in the simultaneous application of:

- *Skill* – the ability to apply technique and do things well, listening and
  influencing effectively;

- *Knowledge and insight* – knowing where to lead; *and*

- *Personal attributes and self-awareness.*

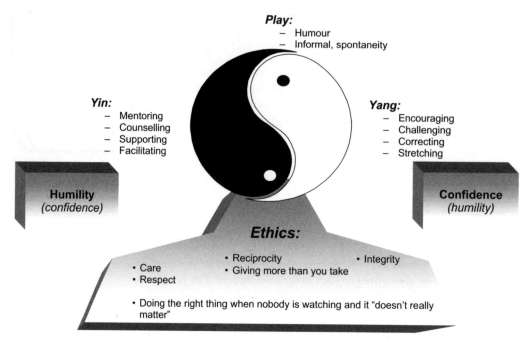

Figure 7.1 Relationship Competence © Yudelowitz, Koch and Field 2002

Yin: mentoring and counseling

The *yin* side of developing other people includes helping them to learn, offering support, acknowledging their individuality, and helping them to transcend their "rackets" (reflex responses to particular events).

The process is non-directive, using "active listening" – paraphrasing, reflecting emotion – and creating a safe journey of discovery, assisting the individual to take charge. The leader needs to be aware of their own rackets and ensure that they don't get in the way.

Mentoring and counseling is characterized by open-mindedness and a non-judgmental attitude. Yet the process is underpinned by an implicit confidence – the leader will take charge if things screw up. This versatility is embedded in the *yin/yang* concept and is noted in our illustration by the small circle of white *(yang)* within the black *(yin)* side of the *yin/yang* symbol.

Yang: coaching and energizing

This is the process of challenging, encouraging and stretching. It includes coaching, advising, and giving feedback

The leader's confidence in providing guidance must be tempered by a degree of humility, accepting that the leader's views may be incomplete or wrong. This is symbolized by the small circle of black *(yin)* within the white *(yang)* side of the *yin/yang* symbol.

What's missing?

The *yin/yang* symbol is apt, but not complete. Strong leadership relationships also require *play* (informality) and *ethics*.

Play

Play – leveraging the informal – is an essential part of building relationships. Play requires letting go, being spontaneous, using humor, or simply laughing together, when two or more people share the odd *meaning* or irony in what happens. If you can see the same thing in the same way and at the same time as a colleague, you celebrate your common humanity – especially useful when relationships have been strained.

Humor says what cannot be said formally, at least without dire consequences. Humor defuses tension. Humor indicates the emergent – what might be, if we look at things differently.

We find that in South Africa, humor in the boardroom or over a meal is very important in helping black and white executives discover one another as people.

Two important caveats, however. Humor cannot be forced. Yet, paradoxically, humor may need to be instantly edited – it can be destructive if it lacks sensitivity and ethics.

Leading is living, and living is meeting

"All real living is meeting ... by the graciousness of its comings, and by the solemn sadness of its goings, the I-thou relationship teaches us to meet others, and to hold our ground when we meet them"

Martin Buber

Ethics

This is the part of the relationship that counts – having integrity and trusting that the other person will act in your interests when nobody is looking. Caring for one another and being committed to each other's growth. Giving more than you take.

Incidentally, avoid excessive politeness. Manners are great, but politeness can stunt relationships. Sadly, politeness is the default style of most leaders. Instead of engaging authentically with others, they interact diplomatically and professionally, avoiding personal risk and possible embarrassment.

If you want to develop deep relationships, engage and connect. Use every minute, every chance encounter, to give other people something useful from your experience and character.

> **Indifference is inhumanity**
>
> "The worst sin to our fellow creatures is not to hate them, but to be indifferent to them; that's the essence of inhumanity"
>
> George Bernard Shaw

Smart quotes

> **Leading is a spontaneous performance**
>
> "Like living itself, leading people is a performing art that is not attained once, but must be created anew and for ever anew"
>
> Otto Rank

Smart quotes

V Leadership is a collective behavior – leadership shared is leadership multiplied

Nearly always in business, there should be one or more individuals unambiguously identified as the leader or leaders. Yet good leaders always encourage and multiply leadership in others. Let's remind ourselves that:

- "No man will make a great leader who wants to do it all himself, or to get all the credit" (Andrew Carnegie);

- "Leadership is best thought of as a behaviour, not a role" (Jill Janov); and

- "The function of leadership is to produce more leaders, not more followers" (Ralph Nader).

Anyone who makes something new and different is a leader, so we can never have too many leaders. Business is change. To make it progress always requires new answers. Every answer is provisional. Eternal innovation and experimentation are the price of staying in business. No individual is going to work it all out. Unless the leader encourages and creates many new leaders, then nothing but the smallest and simplest business can be successfully led. All very successful organizations, that have grown rapidly and conquered the world, have delegated leadership with astonishing verve. Think, for instance, of any religion during its fastest period of expansion.

This *"together"* answer is essential for any top leader who does not have supernatural powers. In the Wheel of Learner Leadership, we have seen, the leader must not only be self-aware, but also learn about what is happening, judge what to do, and act and mobilize the whole enterprise. If the business has any size and complexity, the odds against any one person being able to do it all are prohibitive.

Leaders who thrive know what their strong and weak suits are, and engage other people to help with the latter. Show us a leader who is a great "all-rounder," and we'll show you a leader who is great at self-deception and nothing else. The best leaders are fantastically strong in one area, and arrange that other people take care of all their weak points. Sure, they *know* what needs to be done and can recognize the answer when they see it, but they really need colleagues to sort out *most* of the puzzle.

A lot of nonsense is talked about *"management teams,"* especially *"top management teams."* A team is only really a team if the top person absolutely relies on one or more of the other team members in *most* areas. This is the mark of a strong leader, not a weak one, and most leaders are not strong enough to allow themselves to be truly dependent on other people. Yet without true dependence, leadership is confined to one person, and the organization is immeasurably impoverished.

This, too, is a paradox. Leadership is most evident and effective when the leader *does* the least and exerts leadership through other leaders. Only if the leader truly believes in teamwork – *small* teams where each *individual* has a *different* role – will teams work at all. The leader who does least is most effective. The teams where *each individual leads* are the only effective ones. There is greatest individuality where there is greatest dependence. This is true of all relationships, whether between individuals, people in organizations, or in society generally. The only alternatives to individuality and interdependence are hierarchy or retreat to the hermitage. Neither lead to a flourishing world. Powerful leaders leverage individuality and interdependence, starting with themselves.

A healthy organization is full of people exercising leadership day by day. "Leadership" sounds hierarchical but true leadership is not at all hierarchical. The authority for leadership comes from its quality. If something is said that is self-evidently true, yet points to radical conclusions, then leadership is being exercised, and the level of the person displaying leadership is utterly irrelevant. If the emperor is not wearing clothes, a small boy is enough to cause uproar. If the real decisions are being made by typists and clerks, as in Robin's shipping agency, then they are the leaders. If the chief executive points the wrong way, or is not believed, then there is no leadership.

Leadership means taking responsibility for forcing progress. If people rely on the leader, instead of sorting things out themselves, there will be less progress. The answer lies within – within the individual, within the interdependent small team of individuals. The answer does not lie with the leader, the corporation, the Wizard of Oz, or any other convenient alibi for inaction. Leadership requires individuals to have both freedom, and – what is often more difficult – responsibility.

The statue of "responsibleness"

"Freedom is not the last word. Freedom is only a part of the answer and half of the truth.

"Freedom is but the negative aspect of the whole phenomenon whose positive aspect is 'responsibleness' [sic]. In fact, freedom is in danger of degenerating into mere arbitrariness, unless it is lived in terms of responsibleness.

"That is why I recommend that the Statue of Liberty on the East Coast be supplemented by a Statue of Responsibleness on the West Coast."

Remember the Robert Noyce story? The wise leader sets out the parameters and forces responsible individuals to decide. It's their ass on the line. It's time for them to learn to be leaders.

SMART PEOPLE
TO HAVE ON
YOUR SIDE

MARY PARKER FOLLETT

Political theorist, sociologist, bluestocking social reformer, business writer, feminist, and liberal – meet the amazing Mary Parker Follett (1868–1933). Revered in Japan, ignored in the West until the past ten years, when she has been "rediscovered" – discovered is more apt – she was nothing if not "ahead of her time."

Follett examined creative group processes, crowd psychology, associations, the self in relation to the whole, ideals of integration, synthesis and unifying differences, and relationships in organizations.[7]

What can leaders learn from her?

First, she says leaders, besides coordinating, must define the purpose of the business, and anticipate. "We look to the leader," she writes, "to open up new paths, new opportunities." Anticipation requires seeing the whole picture, the emerging future, even when it is still hazy – the successful leader "sees another picture not yet realized."

Second, she insists that leaders train followers to become leaders. There is no other way to do this, than to trust subordinates and give them scope to make their own decisions: "Responsibility," she said, "is the great developer of men."

Third, the *relationship* between leader and led, and all the other relationships between people in a firm, is crucial. Leading must be a two-way street: Follett argues for "a relation between leaders and led which will give to each the opportunity to make creative contributions to the situation." Ultimately, the hierarchy is less important than the personal relationships between people who work together.

Fourth, she tells us to deal with conflict, to "use it to work for us." There are three ways to resolve conflict – domination, compromise, or integration. Domination and compromise are always flawed. Integration is the only answer. Integration requires us to get behind the ostensible reasons for conflict and "uncover" the real conflict; then to take "the demands of both sides and break them into their constituent parts; then to find a solution that transcends both sides, and integrates the fair requirements of everyone." Avoid the trap of either/or, she tells us. Find something "better than either of two given alternatives."

The final and most important lesson from Mary Parker Follett is one she never wrote about. Contemporary leadership guru, Warren Bennis, notes that she is "dispiritingly identical to contemporary leadership theory." She celebrated non-linearity, opposed command and control, said that front line employees should be incorporated into decision-making, and advocated co-operation, negotiation, constructive conflict, and consensus-making.

Why does Bennis use the word "dispiritingly?" Surely because there is nothing new under the sun, and to work out a brilliant set of theories, based on psychological principles and human wisdom, does not mean that they will be acted upon. Writers can only do so much. Leaders have to do what they say, or there will be no progress. The fact that, on the whole, those in positions of leadership do not follow the generally-agreed best principles of leadership – that a prophet of leadership, who died in 1933, can sound so modern, and have so much to say that is pertinent today – must tell us something hugely important.

What do you think that is? Our explanation is that, whatever we say, the structure of our organizations, and our mind-sets, are still deeply stuck in hierarchical grooves; and that the press of business – the day-to-day demands of management – constantly drive out leadership.

Progress requires the subordination of the urgent to the truly important, the fixation of a suitable top executive on leadership alone, a focus on personal relationships at the expense of roles-based interactions, and the active dismantling of steep and complex structures.

VI   The way we organize for leadership destroys leadership

The way we structure our large organizations, and in particular the way that boards operate and relate to the stock market and investors, make leadership much more difficult than it should be.

In most organizations, formal responsibility for leadership coincides with hierarchy – the leader is the chief executive or the chairman, the top person. Probably, Mr. Big got to the top through skill at management, and, in a publicly listed company, through skill at managing earnings. These skills are not at all those of leadership. Management is about efficient operation of the status quo; leadership is finding and reaching the future.

If we accept this, then there are three corollaries:

- Most leaders are not trained to lead or experienced in leadership. They are probably incompetent in leading. This is not their fault. They are being asked to do something new and difficult without the training for it.

- To have the same person be the chief executive and the chief leader is inappropriate for several reasons. One is that the urgent demands of management today will drive out the less urgent but more important requirements of leadership for tomorrow. Another is that the confusion of leadership with hierarchy makes leadership more difficult – it is more difficult to listen, and more difficult to coach, when you are also the chief executive. A third reason is that leaders need open access to colleagues' hearts and minds, which is made more difficult by the leader's executive power.

- Leadership is a risky enterprise. It ruffles feathers. It often goes wrong. People who want to remain chief executive or chairman are not likely to be bold leaders. They will be tempted to supply the minimum amount of leadership to get by. Besides, they have plenty of other things to worry about.

The problem is made much worse, as Robin has stressed, if the corporation is listed on the stock exchange and the leader is surrounded by professional advisers – accountants, public relations people, investor relations experts, corporate financiers, and even (dare we say) management consultants. Advisers train the corporate head to be cautious, measured, qualified, and to project an image of infallibility – in a phrase, to be economical with leadership. When mistakes are made, they are not used to learn; they are covered up.

The upshot is that by temperament, by training, by the conflict of roles, by the pressure of daily events, by corporate structures, and by calculations of personal gain, the person who is faced with being the leader is also discouraged from exercising full-blooded leadership.

What is to be done?

Individual leaders can try to transcend all these constraints:

- They can ensure that they train themselves properly in leadership.

- They can allocate time for leadership. They can delegate management to a chief operating officer.

- They can multiply leadership by proclaiming their vision and values, and, much more effectively, by living them. They can excite, take risks, admit mistakes, listen, learn, coach, develop, and force everyone to take responsibility for leadership.

- They can tell the board and the stock market the truth, and tell advisers to go to hell.

- They can take a quiet delight in being robust leaders, in defying the system, in being themselves, in having fun. There are plenty of role models to inspire, though not to copy slavishly – Andrew Carnegie, Sam Walton, Bob Noyce, Jack Welch, Percy Barnevik, Richard Branson, Bill Gates.

Yet *structural change* to remove the disincentives for leadership is long overdue. Why tolerate a system that makes leadership – the source of all progress – so very difficult? Why not change it?

We suggest two simple moves:

- Every company appoints a *chief leader*, otherwise known as the *chief leading officer* (CLO). In smaller firms, or in times of tranquility, the CLO might not be a full-time job. The chief executive (CEO) could not also be the CLO. The CEO and CLO would both report to the board of directors, and neither would be more senior. The CLO's job is (1) to make the firm change course when appropriate, and (2) to maximize leadership throughout the organization.

- Each annual report and accounts of large companies includes two reports: one from the chief executive, and one from the chief leader. The CEO's report covers executive matters and the past; the CLO's report deals with the future.

***

Leaders think and reflect, they act and mobilize. We hope we've given you a few high fiber thoughts, a few hints, a few personal challenges. If so, we've done all we can.

Now is the time for you to act, to practice leadership. Whoever you are, you can take responsibility for making the world a richer place. You can do it. Only you can do it your way, with your insights, and your ability to excite other people. Go on. Become the leader that only you can become, and the *best possible* leader that you could become.

Notes

1   Ayn Rand (1938, 1946) *Anthem*, Penguin Putnam, New York.

2   Charles Handy (1994) *The Empty Raincoat: Making Sense of the Future*, Hutchinson, London. Published in the US under the title *The Age of Paradox*.

3   Charles Handy (1986) *Gods of Management*, Souvenir Press, London.

4   Robert Kramer (1995) Carl Rogers meets Otto Rand. In Thierry Pauchent and associates (editors) *In Search of Meaning*, Jossey-Bass, San Francisco.

5   Robert G Eccles and Nitin Nohria (1992) *Beyond the Hype: Rediscovering the Essence of Management*, Harvard Business School Press, Boston.

6   Viktor E. Frankl (1984) Preface to 1984 edition of *Man's Search for Meaning*, Touchstone, New York.

7   Mary Parker Follett (1941) *Dynamic Administration*, edited by Fox, Elliot and Urwick, Lynall, Harper & Bros, New York.

Index

General Electric Company (GEC) 136
General Motors (GM) 70
Gide, André 86
Gleik, James 18
Gödel, Kurt 80
Grey, Sir Edward 122

Haas, Robert 20
Handy, Charles 131, 167–9
Harris, Thomas 56
Hayek, Friedrich von 17
Heisenberg, Werner 80
Henderson, Bruce 30
Heraclitus 6
humor 173–4

Iacocca, Lee 52
individual identity 53
    past and emotions 54–5
    playing games 55–6
    racket club 57–60
insight 144–8, 160
Intel 140

Jackson, Jesse 90
Janov, Jill 33, 175
Jay, Sir Anthony 78

Kissinger, Henry 5, 70
Koch, Richard 104
Koestler, Arthur 22

Kramer, Robert 170

Lao Tsu 51, 73–4
lateral thinking 94–5
leaders
    attributes 38–9
    becoming 48–9
    born or made 40–2
    collective 31–3
    democratic or autocratic 43–4
    described 2–3
    female and outsiders 42–3
    individual 31–3, 182–3
    responsibility 179
    suggestions 183
    tough or gentle 43–4
    work to a purpose 13–14
leadership 22–4
    academically respectable 27
    described 3
    emotional issues 27
    fantasies 51–2
    hype and substance 25–6
    influential 5
    learned 46–8
    necessary 30
    opposite 44–5
    organization 180–2
    personal qualities 5–6
    realities 52–3
    reasons 1–2
    shared and multiplied 175–8